Plant-Based Cookbook for Beginners

130 Easy, Healthy, and Delicious Recipes
To kickstart Your Vegan Journey

Preface

This book is perfect for those who crave vibrant, playful recipes that make cooking easy and plant-based eating an adventure! Its easy, flexible ideas will keep your meals exciting and delicious—just right for a carefree, spontaneous lifestyle. Plus, every dish is a little celebration, just like you!

If you value efficiency and results, this book belongs in your kitchen. Packed with quick, no-fuss recipes, it's designed to save you time while fueling your energy to achieve your goals. It's the perfect tool for your ambitious, success-driven mindset.

For anyone with refined taste and a busy schedule, this is the cookbook you've been waiting for. Each recipe is thoughtfully designed to impress, combining elegant presentation with wholesome flavors that align with your values. It's not just a collection of recipes; it's a lifestyle upgrade for you and your family.

Curious minds who seek the deeper 'why' of plant-based living will find their answer here. This book offers detailed guidance and insights alongside recipes that blend simplicity with depth. It's a meaningful companion on your journey to understanding and growth.

Look no further if you're searching for warmth and ease in the kitchen. This book offers simple, cozy recipes with a touch of creativity—like a warm hug for your soul. It's perfect for quiet moments when you want to infuse magic and imagination into your meals.

This book is a must-have for those who thrive on connection and love to gather people around the table. With approachable recipes and trendy tips, it's ideal for creating meals everyone will enjoy. It's the perfect addition to your vibrant social world.

With all my best,

Virginia Mitchel

Table of Contents

Introduction

Welcome to *Plant-Based Cookbook for Beginners*—a guide designed to help you embrace the transformative power of plant-based eating. I understand that adopting a new way of eating can feel overwhelming. The ongoing uncertainty about what to eat, how to meet nutritional needs, and whether a plant-based lifestyle is sustainable are common challenges for those beginning this journey. Rest assured, this book is here to take the guesswork out of plant-based living, offering simple, practical solutions to make your transition smooth and enjoyable.

I've spent years studying and practicing plant-based nutrition. As an expert in the field, I can confidently say that incorporating more plant-based meals into your life can dramatically improve your health, energy, and overall well-being. Whether you're looking to lose weight, reduce your risk of chronic diseases, or feel better in your everyday life, the benefits of a plant-based diet are profound. By applying the information in this book, you'll be taking a decisive step toward a healthier, more vibrant future.

This cookbook is designed for beginners, busy individuals, families, or anyone curious about adopting a plant-based lifestyle. Whether you're aiming for a complete transition or just looking to incorporate more plant-based meals into your routine, this guide offers simple, delicious recipes to help you get started.

To make your plant-based journey as easy and enjoyable as possible, this book features a variety of recipe categories to suit different needs and occasions, including quick breakfasts, satisfying lunches, comforting dinners, and sweet treats. Each section provides easy-to-follow recipes, perfect for beginners, with practical tips on meal prep, ingredient substitutions, and ways to make plant-based eating simple and fun. Whether cooking for yourself and your family or fitting meals into a busy schedule, these recipes are designed to be accessible, nutritious, and delicious.

Now that you understand the incredible potential of a plant-based lifestyle let's dive into the essentials. In the next chapter, we'll explore the foundational principles of this lifestyle and how easy it can be to incorporate them into your daily routine. Let's start this exciting journey to better health and a more sustainable, fulfilling way of eating.

Part 1. Getting Started

1.1 The Many Benefits of a Plant-Based Diet

Adopting a plant-based diet offers a range of advantages that benefit both personal health and the planet. With its emphasis on whole, natural foods, this way of eating provides a foundation for a healthier, more sustainable lifestyle.

Health Benefits

A plant-based diet is rich in nutrients, fiber, and antioxidants that promote well-being. Studies have shown that it can help reduce the risk of chronic conditions such as heart disease, diabetes, and certain cancers. Additionally, plant-based foods are often lower in calories and saturated fats, making them an excellent choice for maintaining a healthy weight and supporting long-term health.

Hydration of the Body:

Plant-based foods like fruits and vegetables are naturally high in water content, which actively contributes to keeping the body hydrated. Cucumbers, melons, tomatoes, and zucchinis are especially water-rich and help maintain fluid balance, promoting healthy bodily functions and hydrating the skin.

Detoxification:

A plant-based diet supports the body's natural detoxification processes. Plant foods, especially fiber and antioxidants, help the liver and kidneys efficiently remove toxins. Leafy greens, herbs, and various fruits aid in cleansing the body by binding and eliminating harmful substances. The abundance of micronutrients in plant-based foods also supports natural detoxification, leading to greater vitality and overall well-being. These benefits significantly enhance health by nourishing and cleansing the body from the inside out.

Environmental Impact

Beyond personal health, plant-based eating has a significantly lower environmental footprint. Producing plant-based foods requires fewer resources, such as water and land, while generating fewer greenhouse gas emissions than diets centered on animal products. By choosing plant-based meals, individuals can contribute to a more sustainable and eco-friendly future.

Simplicity and Accessibility

One of the greatest appeals of a plant-based diet is its simplicity. Focusing on whole, natural ingredients makes meal preparation straightforward, affordable, and accessible. With versatile options like fresh produce, grains, and legumes, plant-based eating can quickly adapt to various tastes and lifestyles.

1.2 The Plant-Based Lifestyle

A plant-based diet revolves around whole, nutritious foods derived from plants. Focusing on plant-based ingredients provides your body with essential vitamins, minerals, fiber, and antioxidants. The key food groups in a plant-based lifestyle include:

Vegetables

Vegetables form the cornerstone of a plant-based diet. They are rich in vital nutrients, from leafy greens like spinach to cruciferous vegetables such as broccoli and cauliflower. Packed with fiber and antioxidants, vegetables support overall health and provide the body with many vitamins and minerals.

Grains

Whole grains such as quinoa, brown rice, oats, and barley are another essential component of a plant-based diet. These grains are excellent sources of fiber, protein, and complex carbohydrates, providing long-lasting energy while helping to keep you satisfied. Incorporating a variety of grains into your meals ensures a steady supply of nutrients and supports digestive health.

Legumes

Beans, lentils, peas, and chickpeas are powerhouses of protein, fiber, and essential nutrients like iron and folate. They add heartiness to meals and serve as versatile plant-based alternatives to meat. Whether in stews, salads, or veggie burgers, legumes are an excellent way to fuel your body with plant-based protein.

Nuts and Seeds

Nuts and seeds, such as almonds, walnuts, chia seeds, flaxseeds, and pumpkin seeds, are rich in healthy fats, protein, and omega-3 fatty acids. These foods are perfect as snacks or can be added to dishes for extra crunch and nutrition. They provide vital nutrients for heart health, brain function, and well-being.

These food groups create a balanced and varied diet that supports health and boosts energy and well-being. By embracing a plant-based lifestyle, you nourish your body with wholesome, nutrient-dense foods while avoiding animal products, leading to a more vibrant and sustainable way of life.

1.3 Myths Debunked: Plant-Based Eating

Many misconceptions surround plant-based eating, but it's essential to separate fact from fiction. By debunking these myths, we can see how accessible, affordable, and nourishing a plant-based diet truly is. Let's explore and address some of the most common myths:

Myth 1: Plant-Based Diets Lack Protein

One of the most persistent myths about plant-based eating is that it doesn't provide enough protein. Plant-based foods are rich in high-quality protein! Beans, lentils, tofu, tempeh, quinoa, and nuts are all excellent protein sources, offering the building blocks necessary for muscle repair, immune function, and overall health. A varied diet makes it easy to meet your protein needs without relying on animal products. Furthermore, plant proteins have the added benefits of fiber and antioxidants, making them even more nutritious.

Myth 2: Eating Plant-Based is Expensive

Another common misconception is that eating plant-based foods is prohibitively expensive. However, a plant-based diet can be incredibly budget-friendly! Staples like beans, lentils, rice, oats, and frozen vegetables are often much cheaper than meat and dairy products. Plant-based eating becomes even more affordable when you buy in bulk or focus on seasonal produce. With smart shopping, meal prepping, and planning, you can enjoy healthy, plant-based meals without breaking the bank.

Myth 3: Plant-Based Eating is Difficult

Many people believe that transitioning to a plant-based diet is complicated and time-consuming, but this couldn't be further from the truth. Plant-based eating can be straightforward. You can prepare quick, delicious, nutritious meals with essential ingredients like grains, vegetables, and legumes. Many plant-based dishes require minimal preparation; you can make flavorful meals quickly with creativity. This cookbook, for example, features beginner-friendly recipes designed for ease, speed, and convenience—perfect for busy lifestyles.

Myth 4: Plant-Based Diets Are Nutritionally Incomplete

Some critics claim that plant-based diets are nutritionally incomplete, but with careful planning, plant-based eating provides everything your body needs. Plant foods are often richer in essential nutrients like vitamins, minerals, and fiber than animal-based ones. You can quickly meet all your nutritional needs by including a variety of whole foods like leafy greens, legumes, nuts, seeds, and fortified products (like plant-based milks and cereals).

Myth 5: You Can't Get Enough Iron or Calcium on a Plant-Based Diet

Iron and calcium are often cited as nutrients that are hard to obtain without animal products. However, plant-based sources of these nutrients are abundant! Dark leafy greens, legumes, tofu, quinoa, and fortified foods provide ample iron. Options like fortified plant milks, kale, almonds, and broccoli are excellent for calcium. Pairing iron-rich foods with vitamin C (found in citrus fruits and bell peppers) enhances absorption, making it easy to get these essential nutrients without animal-derived foods.

Myth 6: Plant-Based Eating Is Just Salad

Another common myth is that plant-based meals are limited to boring salads. Plant-based eating is incredibly diverse and can

include exciting flavors, textures, and cuisines. The possibilities are endless, from hearty stews and curries to delicious stir-fries, wraps, and baked goods. Plant-based eating is about embracing creativity and variety in the kitchen, using whole foods to craft satisfying meals that nourish the body and the soul.

Plant-based eating is accessible, affordable, and nutrient-dense. By breaking these myths, you can see how easy and enjoyable it is to embrace a healthier, more sustainable way of eating. So, whether you're just starting or looking to incorporate more plant-based meals into your routine, rest assured that a plant-based diet is full of delicious possibilities and lasting benefits.

1.4 Your Plant-Based Pantry and Kitchen

Essential Pantry Staples for Plant-Based Cooking

A well-stocked pantry is the foundation of effortless and flavorful plant-based cooking. Here's what every plant-based pantry needs:

Grains
Stock staples like brown rice, quinoa, oats, bulgur, and whole-grain pasta to serve as the base for countless dishes. For busy days, keep quick-cooking options like couscous or instant rice for speedy meal preparation.

Legumes
Legumes are a powerhouse of protein and fiber, essential for a balanced plant-based diet. Canned or dried beans such as chickpeas, black beans, and kidney beans are pantry essentials. Lentils, split peas, and edamame add variety and can be used in soups, stews, or salads to enhance texture and nutrition.

Spices
Spices and herbs are key to infusing flavor into plant-based dishes. Stock your pantry with essentials like cumin, paprika, turmeric, cinnamon, garlic powder, and chili powder. For versatility, include dried herbs such as oregano, thyme, basil and spice blends like curry powder and garam masala to add depth and global flair to your meals.

Condiments
Condiments bring layers of flavor and texture to plant-based cooking. Soy sauce, tamari, or coconut aminos add a savory depth, while tahini, nut butter, and miso paste create creamy textures and umami notes. Don't forget vinegar (such as apple cider or balsamic) and oils (like olive or sesame) to craft flavorful dressings, marinades, and sauces.

Essential Kitchen Tools for Plant-Based Cooking

Equipping your kitchen with the right tools is key to making plant-based cooking effortless and enjoyable. With just a few essentials, you can streamline meal preparation and confidently tackle everything from simple recipes to complex culinary creations.

Blender
A versatile blender is a cornerstone of plant-based cooking. It's perfect for making smoothies, creamy soups, flavorful sauces, and even homemade nut milk. While high-speed blenders offer exceptional performance, any reliable model will suffice for most tasks.

Food Processor
Save time and effort with a food processor. This versatile tool simplifies the preparation of plant-based staples such as hummus, veggie burgers, energy balls, and shredded vegetables. It's a game-changer for tackling larger meal prep tasks.

Mixing Bowls and Measuring Tools
Accurate measurements are crucial for successful recipes, and a set

of mixing bowls paired with measuring cups and spoons ensures precision. These tools also make mixing, portioning, and preparing ingredients more efficient.

Tips for Ensuring Optimal Nutrient Intake on a Plant-Based Diet

A well-planned plant-based diet can provide all the essential nutrients your body needs to thrive. You can quickly meet your nutritional requirements by focusing on variety and balance. Below are some practical strategies to ensure you're getting key nutrients:

Protein
Protein is essential for muscle repair and overall body function. To meet your protein needs, incorporate beans, lentils, tofu, tempeh, edamame, quinoa, and seitan into your meals—pair grains such as rice with legumes like beans for a complete protein profile.

Iron
Iron supports oxygen transport and energy production in the body. Plant-based sources include spinach, lentils, chickpeas, fortified cereals, and pumpkin seeds. Pair these foods with those rich in vitamin C, such as citrus fruits, bell peppers, and tomatoes, to enhance iron absorption.

Calcium
Calcium is vital for strong bones and teeth, and it can be obtained from fortified plant milk, kale, broccoli, and almonds. Additionally, look for calcium-fortified products like orange juice or cereals to boost your intake.

Vitamin B12
Since vitamin B12 is not naturally present in plant foods, consuming fortified products like shiitake mushrooms and tempeh is essential. Alternatively, a B12 supplement can ensure you meet your daily requirements.

Omega-3 Fatty Acids
Omega-3s contribute to heart and brain health. Great plant-based sources include chia, flaxseeds, walnuts, and hemp seeds. For an additional boost, consider an algae-based omega-3 supplement.

Vitamin D
This nutrient plays a crucial role in bone health and immune function. Aim for 15–20 minutes of sun exposure daily, and include fortified plant-based milk in your diet. If needed, a vitamin D supplement can help maintain optimal levels.

Zinc
Zinc supports immune function and cell repair. To ensure adequate intake, include nuts, seeds (pumpkin and sunflower), chickpeas, and whole grains in your meals.

By incorporating a variety of whole plant foods alongside fortified products, you can confidently meet your nutritional needs while enjoying the benefits of a healthy and balanced diet.

Tips for adjusting the plan for dietary preferences or needs.

One of the significant advantages of plant-based eating is its versatility. This plan is designed to be flexible and easily adaptable to suit various dietary preferences, allergies, or specific health needs. Here are some tips to help you customize the meal plan:

Allergies and Intolerances

> *Gluten-Free:* Substitute gluten-containing grains like whole wheat or orzo with gluten-free alternatives such as quinoa, rice, or gluten-free pasta. Use gluten-free wraps and bread for meals like breakfast burritos or sandwiches.

> *Nut Allergies:* Replace nuts with seeds (e.g., sunflower seeds, pumpkin seeds, or tahini). Use seed-based butter

instead of almond or peanut butter in smoothies and snacks.

Soy Allergies: Swap tofu, tempeh, or soy milk for chickpea tofu, coconut milk, or oat milk. Replace soy sauce with coconut aminos for a similar flavor.

High-Protein Adjustments

To increase your protein intake, incorporate more legumes, lentils, quinoa, seitan, or protein-rich seeds (like hemp, flax, or chia) into meals.

Add plant-based protein powders to smoothies or energy bites for an extra boost.

Low-Carb Preferences

You can replace starchy ingredients like potatoes, rice, or pasta with cauliflower rice, zucchini noodles, or spaghetti squash.

Focus on leafy greens, non-starchy vegetables, and healthy fats like avocado, coconut, and nuts.

Calorie Adjustments

To Increase Calories: Add more nutrient-dense foods such as avocado, nuts, seeds, coconut milk, or nut butter to meals.

To Reduce Calories: Use lower-calorie swaps like unsweetened almond milk, light coconut milk, and steamed or roasted vegetables instead of higher-fat ingredients.

Flavor Preferences

Adjust spices, herbs, and seasonings to match your taste or cultural cuisine preferences. For example, add more garlic and cumin for Mediterranean-inspired flavors or extra ginger and lime for an Asian-inspired twist.

Experiment with the sauces and dressings in the "Sauces, Dips, and Essentials" chapter to tailor dishes to your liking

Meal Timing and Portions

If you follow intermittent fasting or prefer fewer meals, combine snacks with main meals for more significant portions.

Adjust serving sizes based on your hunger levels or energy needs throughout the day.

Seasonal and Budget-Friendly Adjustments

Use fresh, seasonal produce for the best flavor and cost-efficiency. For example, try hearty root vegetables like squash and sweet potatoes in winter, while summer meals might focus on zucchini, tomatoes, and fresh herbs.

Picky Eaters or Family-Friendly Options

Simplify meals by keeping the flavors mild and offering sauces or spices on the side.

Involve family members in selecting and preparing meals to make the plan more enjoyable.

Specialized Diets

Weight Loss Goals: Focus on high-fiber, low-calorie meals like salads, soups, and veggie-based bowls. Minimize oils and caloric sweeteners.

Athletic Performance: Fuel workouts with more high-energy ingredients, such as whole grains, sweet potatoes, and healthy fats.

Plant-based eating is inherently adaptable. The key is to listen to your body, adjust as needed, and embrace the variety and abundance of plant-based foods. Whether you're catering to allergies, preferences, or specific health goals, there's a way to make this plan work beautifully for you!

Part 2. Recipes

Chapter 1: Quick and Easy Breakfasts

Overnight Chia Pudding with Fresh Berries

Prep. time: 5 min   Setting time: 6-8 Hours   Serves: 2

Ingredients

Base:

1/4 cup chia seeds

1 cup almond milk

1 tbsp maple syrup (optional)

1/2 tsp vanilla extract

Topping:

1/2 cup blueberries

1/2 cup sliced strawberries

Optional Add-Ons:

Almond butter, coconut, hemp seeds, granola, or mint

Directions

Mix: Combine chia seeds, almond milk, maple syrup, and vanilla. Whisk well.

Refrigerate: Cover and chill overnight, stirring once in the first hour.

Top: Divide pudding into bowls; add berries and optional topping.

Serving Suggestions:

Serve immediately or cover and keep refrigerated for up to 3 days.

Nutrition (Per Serving)

Calories: 180 | Protein: 6g | Carbs: 23g | Fats: 8g | Fiber: 11g

Avocado and Tomato Breakfast Toast

Prep. time: 10 min   Total time: 10 min   Serves: 2

Ingredients

Two slices of whole-grain or sourdough bread (toasted)

One medium avocado

1/2 tsp lemon juice

Pinch of sea salt and black pepper

Four cherry tomatoes, halved (or one medium tomato, sliced)

1 tbsp fresh basil or parsley, chopped

Optional Add-Ons:

Red pepper flakes, nutritional yeast, hemp seeds, or balsamic glaze

Directions

Toast Bread: Toast bread until golden and crisp.

Mash Avocado: Scoop avocado into a bowl and mash with lemon juice, salt, and pepper.

Assemble Toast: Spread avocado on toast, top with tomatoes, and sprinkle with basil.

Optional Toppings: Add red pepper flakes, hemp seeds, or a drizzle of balsamic glaze for extra flavor

Nutritional Information (Per Serving)

Calories: 220 | Protein: 6 g | Carbs: 26 g | Fats: 13 g

Fiber: 7 g | Sodium: 180 mg | Potassium: 520 mg

5–Minute Banana Oat Pancakes

Prep. time: 5 min   Cook time: 5 min   Serves: 2

Ingredients

One ripe banana
1/2 cup rolled oats
1/4 cup unsweetened almond milk
1/2 tsp baking powder
1/2 tsp cinnamon (optional)
Pinch of salt
Optional Toppings: Fresh fruit, maple syrup, nut butter, or chia seeds

Directions

Blend Batter: Combine banana, oats, almond milk, baking powder, cinnamon, and salt in a blender. Blend until smooth.
Cook Pancakes: Heat a non-stick pan over medium heat. Pour small amounts of batter into each pancake. Cook for 2–3 minutes per side until golden brown.

Serving Suggestions:
Top with fresh fruit, maple syrup, or nut butter

Nutrition (Per Serving)

Calories: 200 | Protein: 5g | Carbs: 38g | Fats: 3g | Fiber: 6g

Plant-Based Breakfast Burrito with Tofu Scramble

Prep. time: 10 min   Cook time: 10 min   Serves: 2

Ingredients

Tofu Scramble:
One block (14 oz) of firm tofu, crumbled
1 tbsp olive oil
1/2 tsp turmeric
1/2 tsp garlic powder
1/4 tsp black salt (kala namak, optional for "eggy" flavor)
Salt and pepper to taste
1/2 cup diced bell peppers
1/4 cup chopped onion
1/4 cup spinach
Assembly:
Two large whole-grain tortillas
1/4 cup avocado slices
2 tbsp salsa
Optional Add-Ons: Black beans, vegan cheese, or hot sauce

Directions

Prepare Tofu Scramble: Heat oil in a skillet over medium heat. Sauté onion and peppers until softened. Add crumbled tofu, turmeric, garlic powder, and black salt. Cook for 5 minutes, stirring, then mix in spinach.
Assemble the Burrito: Place the tofu scramble on a tortilla, add the avocado and salsa, and fold it into a burrito.

Serving Suggestions:
Warm in a skillet for a crispy finish, or enjoy as is.

Nutrition (Per Serving)

Calories: 300 | Protein: 15g | Carbs: 30g | Fats: 12g | Fiber: 6g

Creamy Coconut Yogurt Parfaits

Prep. time: 15 min   Setting time: 15 min   Serves: 4

Ingredients

Coconut Yogurt Base
2 cups unsweetened coconut yogurt
2 tbsp maple syrup (optional)
1 tsp vanilla extract
Fruit Layer
1 cup fresh mixed berries (strawberries, blueberries, raspberries)
One banana, sliced
Topping
1 cup plant-based granola
Optional Add-Ons
2 tbsp chia or flaxseeds
2 tbsp chopped nuts or shredded coconut

Directions

Mix Yogurt Base: Combine coconut yogurt, maple syrup, and vanilla in a bowl. Stir until smooth.
Layer Parfaits: In jars, alternate layers of yogurt, fruit, and granola. Add optional toppings like seeds or nuts for more nutrients.
Chill (Optional): Cover and refrigerate for 15 minutes for a refreshing parfait.
Serve: Enjoy immediately or store covered for up to 24 hours in the refrigerator.

Serving Suggestions:
Pair with tea or coffee for breakfast or drizzled dark chocolate for dessert.

Nutritional Info (Per Serving):
Calories: 220 | Protein: 5g | Carbs: 35g | Fats: 9g
Fiber: 5g | Cholesterol: 0mg | Sodium: 35mg | Potassium: 280mg

High-Protein Peanut Butter Smoothie Bowl

Prep. time: 10 min   Total time: 10 min   Serves: 2

Ingredients

Smoothie Base:
Two frozen bananas
1 cup unsweetened almond milk
2 tbsp peanut butter
One scoop of plant-based protein powder
1 tbsp chia seeds
Optional Toppings:
½ cup granola
2 tbsp chopped nuts or seeds (e.g., almonds, pumpkin seeds)
1 tbsp shredded coconut
1 tbsp cacao nibs or dark chocolate chips
Fresh fruit slices (e.g., banana, berries)

Directions

Prepare Smoothie Base:
Combine frozen bananas, almond milk, peanut butter, protein powder, and chia seeds in a blender. Blend until thick and creamy. Add more milk if needed to adjust consistency.
Assemble the Bowl:
Divide the smoothie between two bowls.
Adding toppings of your choice, such as granola, fresh fruit, or seeds, can enhance the flavor and nutrients.
Serve: Enjoy immediately for a refreshing, high-protein meal.

Nutritional Info (Per Serving):
Calories: 350 | Protein: 18g | Carbs: 45g | Fats: 12g
Fiber: 8g | Cholesterol: 0mg | Sodium: 180mg | Potassium: 600mg

Fluffy Vegan Apple Cinnamon Muffins

Prep. time: 15 min   Bake time: 20-25 min   Serves: 12

Ingredients

Dry Ingredients:

1 ¾ cup whole wheat or all-purpose flour

1 tsp baking powder

½ tsp baking soda

1 tsp cinnamon

¼ tsp nutmeg

¼ tsp salt

Wet Ingredients:

1 cup unsweetened applesauce

⅓ cup maple syrup

⅓ cup coconut oil (melted) or neutral oil

1 tsp vanilla extract

½ cup plant-based milk (e.g., almond, oat)

Add-Ins:

One small apple, finely diced

¼ cup chopped walnuts or raisins (optional)

Directions

Preheat Oven: Set oven to 350°F (175°C). Line a muffin tin with paper liners or lightly grease it.

Mix Dry Ingredients: In a large bowl, whisk together flour, baking powder, baking soda, cinnamon, nutmeg, and salt.

Prepare Wet Ingredients: In a separate bowl, combine applesauce, maple syrup, melted coconut oil, vanilla extract, and plant-based milk. Mix until smooth.

Combine: Gradually add the wet ingredients to the dry, stirring gently. Avoid overmixing. Fold in diced apple and optional add-ins.

Bake: Divide batter evenly among the muffin cups. Bake for 20–25 minutes or until a toothpick inserted in the center comes clean.

Cool: Let muffins cool in the tin for 5 minutes before transferring to a wire rack.

Serving Suggestions: Serve warm with vegan butter or nut butter. Pair with coffee or tea for a cozy snack.

Nutritional Info (Per Muffin):

Calories: 170 | Protein: 2.5g | Carbs: 24g | Fats: 7g

Fiber: 2g | Cholesterol: 0mg | Sodium: 115mg | Potassium: 110mg

Savory Sweet Potato Breakfast Hash

Prep. time: 10 min   Cook time: 25 min   Serves: 4

Ingredients

Two medium sweet potatoes, diced (about 3 cups)

1 tbsp olive oil or avocado oil

One small red onion, diced

One bell pepper (any color), diced

1 cup cooked black beans (or chickpeas)

1 tsp smoked paprika

1 tsp garlic powder

½ tsp ground cumin

Salt and pepper to taste

2 cups fresh spinach or kale, chopped

Optional Toppings:

Sliced avocado

Hot sauce or salsa

Fresh herbs (cilantro, parsley)

Directions

Prepare Sweet Potatoes: Steam or microwave sweet potatoes for 5–7 minutes to soften slightly.

Cook the Hash: Heat oil in a large skillet over medium heat. Add sweet potatoes and cook until golden, about 8–10 minutes. Stir in onion, bell pepper, and spices. Cook for another 5–7 minutes, stirring occasionally.

Add Beans and Greens: Mix in black beans and cook for 2 minutes. Add spinach or kale and stir until wilted.

Serving Suggestions:

Plate the hash and top with avocado, hot sauce, or your favorite toppings.

Nutritional Info (Per Serving):

Calories: 230 | Protein: 6g | Carbs: 36g | Fats: 6g

Fiber: 8g | Cholesterol: 0mg | Sodium: 150mg | Potassium: 750mg

Instant Pot Steel-Cut Oats with Maple and Walnuts

Prep. time: 5 min   Cook time: 25 min   Serves: 4

Ingredients

1 cup steel-cut oats
3 cups water or unsweetened plant milk (e.g., almond, oat)
1 tsp cinnamon
¼ tsp salt
2 tbsp maple syrup (plus more for drizzling)
¼ cup chopped walnuts
Optional Toppings and Variations:
Fresh fruit (e.g., banana slices, berries)
1 tbsp chia seeds or hemp seeds
Shredded coconut or cacao nibs
A dollop of almond butter

Directions

Prepare the Oats: Rinse the oats under cold water to remove excess starch (optional for a creamier texture).
Cook in Instant Pot: Add oats, water or plant milk, cinnamon, and salt to the Instant Pot. Secure the lid and set it to "Pressure Cook" or "Manual" for 10 minutes. Allow natural pressure release for 10 minutes, then carefully quickly release any remaining pressure.
Mix in Sweetener and Nuts: Stir in maple syrup and chopped walnuts.
Serve: Divide into bowls and top with optional toppings. Drizzle with additional maple syrup if desired.

Nutritional Info (Per Serving):

Calories: 210 | Protein: 6g | Carbs: 30g | Fats: 7g
Fiber: 5g | Cholesterol: 0mg | Sodium: 120mg | Potassium: 180mg

Quick Tropical Green Smoothie

Prep. time: 5 min   Total time: 5 min   Serves: 2

Ingredients

1 cup fresh spinach, packed
1 cup frozen mango chunks
One frozen banana
1 cup unsweetened coconut water or plant-based milk
One tablespoon of chia or flaxseeds
Juice of ½ lime
Optional Toppings or Variations:
Hemp seeds
Shredded coconut
Fresh mint
Sliced kiwi or pineapple

Directions

Add spinach, mango, banana, coconut water, seeds, and lime juice to a blender.
Blend on high until smooth. Add more liquid if needed for the desired consistency.
Pour into glasses and garnish with toppings as desired.
Serving Suggestions:
Enjoy immediately as a refreshing breakfast or snack.

Nutritional Info (Per Serving):

Calories: 140 | Protein: 3g | Carbs: 30g | Fats: 2g
Fiber: 4g | Cholesterol: 0mg | Sodium: 25mg | Potassium: 400 mg

Golden Glow Turmeric Spiced Oats

Prep. time: 5 min   Total time: 10 min   Serves: 2

Ingredients

rolled oats 1 cup
unsweetened almond milk or water 2 cups
ground turmeric 1/2 tsp
ground cinnamon 1/2 tsp
ground ginger 1/4 tsp
Maple syrup 1 tbsp (optional)
vanilla extract 1/2 tsp
pinch of black pepper
pinch of salt
Optional Toppings
sliced banana
toasted nuts or seeds (almonds, walnuts, chia seeds)
shredded coconut
fresh berries
Drizzle of almond butter

Directions

Cook Oats: Combine the rolled oats and almond milk in a medium saucepan over medium heat. Stir occasionally and bring to a gentle simmer.

Add Spices: Stir in ground turmeric, cinnamon, ginger, black pepper, and salt. Mix well to distribute the spices evenly.

Sweeten and Flavor: Once the oats thicken, add the maple syrup (if using) and vanilla extract. Stir to combine and cook for an additional 2 minutes.

Serve: Spoon the spiced oats into bowls. Top with banana slices, nuts, seeds, or any of your favorite toppings for added flavor and nutrition.

Nutritional Info (Per Serving)

Calories: 180 | Protein: 3g | Carbs: 16g | Fats: 13g
Fiber: 4g | Cholesterol: 0mg | Sodium: 600mg | Potassium: 550mg

Golden Glow Turmeric Spiced Oats make a warm and comforting breakfast. They are packed with turmeric and ginger's anti-inflammatory benefits, perfect for starting your day with nourishing, plant-based energy.

Berry Bliss Smoothie and Granola Jar

Prep. time: 10 min   Total time: 10 min   Serves: 2

Ingredients

frozen mixed berries 1 cup
banana one medium
unsweetened almond milk 1 cup
unsweetened plant-based yogurt 1/2 cup
rolled oats or granola 1/2 cup
chia seeds 1 tbsp
vanilla extract 1/2 tsp
Maple syrup 1 tbsp (optional)
Optional Toppings
sliced fresh fruit
shredded coconut
crushed nuts or seeds (almonds, flaxseeds)

Directions

Blend Smoothie: Add frozen mixed berries, banana, almond milk, plant-based yogurt, vanilla extract, and maple syrup (if using) to a blender. Blend until smooth and creamy.

Prepare Jar: Spoon a layer of granola or oats into the bottom of a jar or bowl. Add a layer of the blended smoothie mixture.

Layer: Alternate layers of granola and smoothie until the jar is full.

Top: Garnish with additional granola, sliced fresh fruit, and a sprinkle of shredded coconut or nuts for added texture and flavor.

Serve: Enjoy immediately with a spoon for a delicious and nutrient-packed breakfast or snack.

Nutritional Info (Per Serving)

Calories: 180 | Protein: 3g | Carbs: 16g | Fats: 13g
Fiber: 4g | Cholesterol: 0mg | Sodium: 600mg | Potassium: 550mg

The Berry Bliss Smoothie and Granola Jar combines antioxidant-rich berries with wholesome oats for a refreshing and satisfying plant-based meal. Perfect for meal prep or on-the-go mornings!

Sweet and Savory Nut Butter Breakfast Crostini

Prep. time: 10 min   Total time: 10 min   Serves: 4

Ingredients

sliced whole-grain baguette eight slices (about 1/2 inch thick)
almond or peanut butter 1/4 cup
Banana 1 medium, sliced thin.
avocado 1/2, mashed
chia seeds 1 tsp
hemp seeds 1 tsp
Maple syrup 1 tbsp (optional)
sea salt a pinch
Optional Toppings
mixed berries
sliced nuts (almonds, walnuts)
microgreens or arugula

Directions

Toast Bread: Lightly toast the baguette slices until golden and crisp.
Spread Nut Butter: Spread almond or peanut butter on half the toasted slices.
Add Sweet Topping: Top the nut butter with banana slices, a drizzle of maple syrup (if using), and a sprinkle of chia seeds.
Spread Avocado: Mash the avocado and spread it on the remaining toasted slices.
Add Savory Topping: For a savory kick, garnish the avocado crostini with hemp seeds, sea salt, and optional microgreens or arugula.
Serve: Arrange on a plate and enjoy immediately as a balanced, nutrient-rich breakfast or snack.

Nutritional Info (Per Serving)

Calories: 180 | Protein: 3g | Carbs: 16g | Fats: 13g
Fiber: 4g | Cholesterol: 0mg | Sodium: 600mg | Potassium: 550mg
The Sweet and Savory Nut Butter Breakfast Crostini offers a delightful contrast of flavors and textures. It provides a wholesome start to your day with healthy fats, fiber, and natural sweetness!

Zesty Lemon Poppy Seed Vegan Muffins

Prep. time: 15 min   Bake time: 20 min   Serves: 12

Ingredients

all-purpose flour 2 cups
cane sugar 3/4 cup
baking powder 1 1/2 tsp
baking soda 1/2 tsp
salt 1/4 tsp
unsweetened almond milk 3/4 cup
lemon juice 1/4 cup (freshly squeezed)
lemon zest 1 tbsp
unsweetened applesauce 1/3 cup
neutral oil (e.g., sunflower or avocado) 1/3 cup
vanilla extract 1 tsp
poppy seeds 2 tbsp
Optional Toppings
sliced almonds
lemon glaze (powdered sugar and lemon juice mix)

Directions

Preheat Oven: Preheat your oven to 350°F (175°C). Line a muffin tin with paper liners or lightly grease it.
Mix Dry Ingredients: In a large bowl, whisk together the flour, sugar, baking powder, baking soda, salt, and poppy seeds.
Combine Wet Ingredients: In a separate bowl, mix almond milk, lemon juice, lemon zest, applesauce, oil, and vanilla extract. Let the lemon juice sit for 1-2 minutes to curdle the almond milk slightly.
Combine and Fold: Gradually add the wet ingredients to the dry ingredients. Gently fold until just combined. Avoid overmixing.
Fill Muffin Tin: Divide the batter evenly among the muffin cups, filling each about three-quarters full.
Bake Muffins: Bake for 18-20 minutes or until a toothpick inserted into the center comes out clean.
Cool: Let the muffins cool in the tin for 5 minutes, then transfer them to a wire rack to cool completely.
Serve: Enjoy plain or drizzle with a simple lemon glaze and sprinkle with sliced almonds for extra texture.

Nutritional Info (Per Serving)

Calories: 180 | Protein: 3g | Carbs: 16g | Fats: 13g
Fiber: 4g | Cholesterol: 0mg | Sodium: 600mg | Potassium: 550mg

Chapter 2: Satisfying Snacks and Smoothies

Crispy Baked Chickpeas with Spices

Prep. time: 10 min   Setting time: 30-40 min   Serves: 4

Ingredients

2 cups cooked chickpeas (or one can, drained and rinsed)

1 tbsp olive oil

1 tsp paprika

1 tsp cumin

1/2 tsp garlic powder

1/4 tsp turmeric (optional)

Salt and pepper, to taste

1 tbsp lemon juice (optional)

Toppings (optional):

Fresh parsley or cilantro

A sprinkle of nutritional yeast for a cheesy flavor

Directions

Preheat the oven to 400°F (200°C).

Prepare chickpeas: Pat chickpeas dry with a towel to remove excess moisture. This helps them crisp up.

Seasoning: Toss chickpeas with olive oil, paprika, cumin, garlic powder, turmeric, salt, and pepper in a bowl.

Bake: Spread the chickpeas on a baking sheet in a single layer. Bake for 25-30 minutes, shaking the pan halfway through, until golden and crispy.

Optional: Drizzle with lemon juice after baking and garnish with fresh herbs or nutritional yeast for added flavor.

Serving Suggestions:

Serve as a snack, salad topping, or side dish with hummus or a plant-based dip.

Nutritional Info (Per Serving):

Calories: 140 | Protein: 7g | Carbs: 22g | Fats: 5g

Fiber: 6g | Cholesterol: 0mg | Sodium: 200mg | Potassium: 400 mg

Cashew Cheese and Veggie Sticks

Prep. time: 15 min   Setting time: 30 min   Serves: 4

Ingredients

For the Cashew Cheese:

1 cup raw cashews (soaked for 2-4 hours)

2 tbsp nutritional yeast

1 tbsp lemon juice

1/4 cup water (adjust for desired consistency)

1/2 tsp garlic powder

1/4 tsp salt

1/4 tsp turmeric (optional)

For the Veggie Sticks:

Two carrots, cut into sticks

One cucumber cut into sticks

One bell pepper, cut into sticks

One celery stalk, cut into sticks

Directions

Soak Cashews: If using raw cashews, soak them in water for 2-4 hours or overnight to soften.

Make Cashew Cheese: Drain cashews and blend with nutritional yeast, lemon juice, garlic powder, salt, turmeric, and water until smooth and creamy. Adjust the water to achieve the desired consistency.

Prepare Veggie Sticks: Cut carrots, cucumbers, bell peppers, and celery into equal-sized sticks for easy dipping.

Serve: Arrange veggie sticks on a plate with cashew cheese on the side for dipping.

Toppings/Variations (optional):

Add fresh herbs (parsley or dill) to the cashew cheese for extra flavor.

Spice it up with a pinch of cayenne or smoked paprika.

Serving Suggestions:

Serve with a fresh salad as a snack, appetizer, or side dish. Perfect for dipping!

Nutritional Info (Per Serving):

Calories: 180 | Protein: 5g | Carbs: 15g | Fats: 12g

Fiber: 3g | Cholesterol: 0mg | Sodium: 140mg | Potassium: 450 mg

Zesty Avocado Hummus Dip

Prep. time: 10 min   Total time: 10 min   Serves: 4

Ingredients

One ripe avocado
1 cup cooked chickpeas (or one can, drained and rinsed)
2 tbsp tahini
2 tbsp lemon juice
One clove garlic
1/2 tsp cumin
1/4 tsp salt (adjust to taste)
1/4 tsp paprika (optional, for garnish)
2 tbsp water (adjust for consistency)
Optional Add-ons:
A drizzle of olive oil or sprinkle of chili flakes for garnish
Fresh cilantro or parsley for a herbaceous touch

Directions

Prepare Ingredients: If using canned chickpeas, rinse them well to reduce sodium.
Blend: Combine avocado, chickpeas, tahini, lemon juice, garlic, cumin, salt, and water in a blender or food processor. Blend until smooth, scraping down sides as needed. Adjust the water for a creamier texture.
Garnish: Transfer to a serving bowl, drizzle with olive oil, and sprinkle with paprika or chili flakes. Add fresh herbs if desired.
Serve: Pair with veggie sticks, whole-grain crackers, or pita bread.

Nutritional Info (Per Serving):

Calories: 160 | Protein: 4g | Carbs: 15g | Fats: 10g
Fiber: 6g | Cholesterol: 0mg | Sodium: 120mg | Potassium: 480 mg

No-Bake Energy Bites with Dates and Cacao

Prep. time: 15 min   Setting time: 15 min   Serves: 4 (12 Bites)

Ingredients

1 cup pitted dates (soaked for 10 minutes if dry)
1/2 cup rolled oats
2 tbsp cacao powder
2 tbsp almond butter (or peanut butter)
1/4 cup chopped nuts (almonds or walnuts)
1 tbsp chia seeds (optional)
1/2 tsp vanilla extract
Optional Add-ons:
A pinch of sea salt
Shredded coconut for rolling

Directions

Prepare Dates: If dates are dry, soak in warm water for 10 minutes and drain.
Blend Ingredients: In a food processor, blend dates until they form a paste. Add oats, cacao powder, almond butter, nuts, chia seeds, vanilla, and salt. Blend until the mixture is combined and sticky.
Form Bites: Roll the mixture into 12 equal-sized balls. Optionally, roll in shredded coconut for added texture.
Set: Refrigerate for 15 minutes to firm up or enjoy immediately.

Serving Suggestions:
It's perfect as a snack, pre- or post-workout fuel, or a healthy dessert. Store it in the fridge for up to a week.

Nutritional Info (Per Serving - 3 bites)

Calories: 180 | Protein: 4g | Carbs: 25g | Fats: 7g
Fiber: 5g | Cholesterol: 0mg | Sodium: 20mg | Potassium: 350 mg

Air-Fried Sweet Potato Wedges

Prep. time: 10 min   Cook time: 15 min   Serves: 4

Ingredients

Two large, sweet potatoes (about 1 lb), cut into wedges
1 tbsp olive oil
1/2 tsp paprika
1/2 tsp garlic powder
1/4 tsp cumin
1/4 tsp salt (optional)
1/4 tsp black pepper
Optional Add-ons:
Sprinkle of chili flakes for spice
Fresh parsley or cilantro for garnish

Directions

Prepare Sweet Potatoes: Wash sweet potatoes thoroughly. Cut into wedges, keeping them uniform for even cooking.
Season: Toss wedges in olive oil, paprika, garlic powder, cumin, salt, and pepper to coat evenly.
Air-Fry: Preheat the air fryer to 375°F (190°C). Arrange the wedges in a single layer in the basket. Cook for 12-15 minutes, shaking the basket halfway, until crispy and golden.
Serve: Garnish with fresh herbs or chili flakes if desired.

Nutritional Info (Per Serving):

Calories: 130 | Protein: 2g | Carbs: 22g | Fats: 4g
Fiber: 3g | Cholesterol: 0mg | Sodium: 80mg | Potassium: 380 mg

Classic Plant-Based Trail Mix

Prep. time: 5 min   Total time: 5 min   Serves: 8

Ingredients

1 cup raw almonds
1 cup raw cashews
1/2 cup sunflower seeds
1/2 cup pumpkin seeds
1/2 cup dried cranberries (unsweetened)
1/2 cup raisins
1/3 cup dark chocolate chips (dairy-free)
1/4 tsp sea salt (optional)
Optional Add-ons:
1/4 cup shredded coconut
1/4 cup goji berries or other dried fruits

Directions

Combine Ingredients: In a large bowl, mix almonds, cashews, sunflower seeds, pumpkin seeds, dried cranberries, raisins, chocolate chips, and optional add-ons.
Season: Sprinkle with sea salt if desired.
Store: Transfer to an airtight container for freshness.

Serving Suggestions:
Enjoy as a snack, hiking fuel, or sprinkle on smoothie bowls or oatmeal.

Nutritional Info (Per Serving - ~1/4 cup):

Calories: 200 | Protein: 5g | Carbs: 20g | Fats: 12g
Fiber: 3g | Cholesterol: 0mg | Sodium: 10mg | Potassium: 250 mg

Creamy Mango Lassi (Dairy-Free)

Prep. time: 5 min   Total time: 5 min   Serves: 2

Ingredients

One large ripe mango (or 1 cup frozen mango chunks)

1/2 cup unsweetened coconut yogurt

1/2 cup unsweetened almond milk (or plant milk of choice)

1 tbsp maple syrup (optional, adjust to taste)

1/4 tsp cardamom powder

2-3 ice cubes

Optional Add-ons:

A pinch of saffron for richness

A sprinkle of chopped pistachios or shredded coconut for garnish

Directions

Prepare mango: Peel and dice fresh mango if you are using it.

Blend: Combine mango, coconut yogurt, almond milk, maple syrup, cardamom, and ice cubes in a blender. Blend until smooth and creamy.

Serve: Pour into glasses and garnish with pistachios or coconut if desired.

Serving Suggestions:

Enjoy as a refreshing snack, breakfast drink, or light dessert.

Nutritional Info (Per Serving):

Calories: 150 | Protein: 2g | Carbs: 30g | Fats: 4g

Fiber: 3g | Cholesterol: 0mg | Sodium: 20mg | Potassium: 300 mg

Berry Blast Protein Smoothie

Prep. time: 5 min   Total time: 5 min   Serves: 2

Ingredients

1 cup mixed berries (fresh or frozen)

One medium banana

One scoop of plant-based protein powder (vanilla or unflavored)

1 cup unsweetened almond milk (or plant milk of choice)

1 tbsp chia seeds

1 tbsp almond butter (optional for creaminess)

2-3 ice cubes (optional for a thicker smoothie)

Optional Add-ons:

A pinch of cinnamon

A handful of spinach for added green

Directions

Blend: Combine berries, banana, protein powder, almond milk, chia seeds, and almond butter in a blender. Add ice if desired. Blend until smooth.

Serve: Pour into glasses and garnish with fresh berries or a sprinkle of chia seeds.

Nutritional Info (Per Serving):

Calories: 190 | Protein: 10g | Carbs: 25g | Fats: 6g

Fiber: 6g | Cholesterol: 0mg | Sodium: 120mg | Potassium: 400 mg

Garlic and Herb Kale Chips

Prep. time: 10 min   Cook time: 15 min   Serves: 4

Ingredients

One large bunch of kale (about 6 cups, stems removed, leaves torn)
1 tbsp olive oil
1 tsp garlic powder
1/2 tsp onion powder
1/2 tsp dried thyme or oregano
1/4 tsp salt
1/4 tsp black pepper
Optional Add-ons:
2 tbsp nutritional yeast for a cheesy flavor
A pinch of chili flakes for heat

Directions

Preheat Oven: Set oven to 300°F (150°C).
Prepare Kale: Wash and thoroughly dry kale (moisture prevents crispiness).
Season: Toss kale with olive oil, garlic powder, onion powder, herbs, salt, and pepper in a large bowl, ensuring even coating.
Bake: Spread kale in a single layer on a baking sheet. Bake for 10-15 minutes, checking frequently to avoid burning.
Cool: Let chips cool on the tray for maximum crunch.

Serving Suggestions:
Enjoy as a snack or pair with a plant-based dip for a light appetizer. Perfect for meal prep!

Nutritional Info (Per Serving):
Calories: 70 | Protein: 2g | Carbs: 7g | Fats: 4g
Fiber: 2g | Cholesterol: 0mg | Sodium: 120mg | Potassium: 350 mg

Decadent Chocolate Peanut Butter Smoothie

Prep. time: 5 min   Total time: 5 min   Serves: 2

Ingredients

One large frozen banana
1 cup unsweetened almond milk (or plant milk of choice)
2 tbsp natural peanut butter
1 tbsp cacao powder (or unsweetened cocoa powder)
1 scoop plant-based chocolate protein powder (optional)
1 tsp maple syrup (optional, adjust to taste)
2-3 ice cubes (optional)
Optional Add-ons:
A pinch of cinnamon
1 tbsp chia seeds or flaxseeds for added nutrition

Directions

Blend: Combine banana, almond milk, peanut butter, cacao powder, protein powder (if using), maple syrup, and ice in a blender. Blend until creamy and smooth.
Serve: Pour into glasses and top with a sprinkle of cacao nibs, chopped peanuts, or a drizzle of peanut butter for garnish.

Serving Suggestions:
Enjoy as a post-workout shake, dessert alternative, or a satisfying snack.

Nutritional Info (Per Serving):
Calories: 220 | Protein: 7g | Carbs: 26g | Fats: 10g
Fiber: 4g | Cholesterol: 0mg | Sodium: 100mg | Potassium: 450 mg

Crunchy Roasted Edamame Bites

Prep. time: 5 min   Total time: 20 min   Serves: 4

Ingredients

frozen shelled edamame 2 cups (thawed)
olive oil 1 tbsp
garlic powder 1/2 tsp
paprika 1/2 tsp
sea salt 1/4 tsp
black pepper 1/4 tsp
Optional Toppings
nutritional yeast for a cheesy flavor
red chili flakes for added spice

Directions

Preheat Oven: Preheat your oven to 400°F (200°C). Line a baking sheet with parchment paper.
Prepare Edamame: Pat the thawed edamame dry with a clean kitchen towel to remove excess moisture.
Season: In a mixing bowl, toss the edamame with olive oil, garlic powder, paprika, salt, and pepper until evenly coated.
Bake: Spread the seasoned edamame in a single layer on the prepared baking sheet. Bake for 18-20 minutes, stirring halfway through, until golden and crispy.
Cool: Remove from the oven and let cool slightly to crisp up further.
Serve: Enjoy as a high-protein snack or add to salads and grain bowls for extra crunch. Sprinkle with nutritional yeast or red chili flakes if desired.

Nutritional Info (Per Serving)

Calories: 180 | Protein: 12g | Carbs: 13g | Fats: 7g
Fiber: 5g | Cholesterol: 0mg | Sodium: 290mg | Potassium: 450mg
Crunchy Roasted Edamame Bites are a savory, satisfying snack that's easy to make and packed with plant-based protein and fiber!

Tropical Pineapple Coconut Protein Smoothie

Prep. time: 5 min   Total time: 5 min   Serves: 2

Ingredients

frozen pineapple chunks 2 cups
unsweetened coconut milk 1 cup
plant-based vanilla protein powder, two scoops
banana one medium (optional for creaminess)
chia seeds 1 tsp
unsweetened shredded coconut 1 tbsp (plus extra for topping)
ice cubes 1/2 cup
Optional Toppings
fresh pineapple slices
toasted coconut flakes
hemp seeds for added nutrition

Directions

Blend Ingredients: Add frozen pineapple chunks, coconut milk, protein powder, banana (if using), chia seeds, shredded coconut, and ice cubes to a high-speed blender. Blend until smooth and creamy.
Adjust Consistency: If the smoothie is too thick, add more coconut milk until it reaches the desired consistency.
Serve: Pour into glasses and top with fresh pineapple slices, toasted coconut flakes, or hemp seeds for an extra boost of flavor and nutrition.
Enjoy: Serve immediately as a refreshing and protein-packed breakfast or post-workout snack.

Nutritional Info (Per Serving)

Calories: 190 | Protein: 10g | Carbs: 22g | Fats: 8g
Fiber: 4g | Cholesterol: 0mg | Sodium: 150mg | Potassium: 600mg
This Tropical Pineapple Coconut Protein Smoothie is a vibrant, energizing drink perfect for fueling your day!

Spicy Black Bean Dip with Lime

Prep. time: 10 min   Total time: 10 min   Serves: 4

Ingredients

black beans (cooked or canned, drained and rinsed) 2 cups
lime juice 2 tbsp
olive oil 2 tbsp
garlic cloves 2 minced
jalapeño one small (seeded for less heat, optional)
ground cumin 1 tsp
smoked paprika 1 tsp
salt 1/2 tsp
fresh cilantro 1/4 cup chopped (plus extra for garnish)
water 2–3 tbsp (adjust for consistency)
Optional Toppings
diced tomatoes
sliced green onions
extra lime wedges

Directions

Blend Ingredients: Add black beans, lime juice, olive oil, garlic, jalapeño, cumin, smoked paprika, salt, and cilantro to a food processor.
Adjust Consistency: Blend while adding water until the dip reaches your desired smoothness.
Taste and Adjust: Taste and add more lime juice, salt, or spices if needed.
Serve: Transfer to a serving bowl and garnish with diced tomatoes, green onions, or extra cilantro.
Pair: Serve with tortilla chips and veggie sticks or spread in wraps and sandwiches.

Nutritional Info (Per Serving)

Calories: 160 | Protein: 6g | Carbs: 18g | Fats: 6g
Fiber: 7g | Cholesterol: 0mg | Sodium: 450mg | Potassium: 480mg
This Spicy Black Bean Dip with Lime is zesty, wholesome, and perfect for dipping or spreading!

Refreshing Cucumber Mint Smoothie

Prep. time: 5 min   Total time: 5 min   Serves: 2

Ingredients

cucumber (peeled and chopped) 1 large
Fresh mint leaves 1/4 cup.
unsweetened almond milk 1 cup
frozen pineapple chunks 1/2 cup
banana (ripe) 1
lime juice 1 tbsp
ice cubes 1 cup
Maple syrup 1 tsp (optional, for added sweetness)
Optional Toppings
chia seeds
cucumber slices
fresh mint sprigs

Directions

Blend Ingredients: Add cucumber, mint leaves, almond milk, pineapple, banana, lime juice, and ice cubes to a blender.
Sweeten: If a sweeter flavor is desired, add maple syrup. Blend until smooth and creamy.
Serve: Pour into glasses and garnish with chia seeds, cucumber slices, or fresh mint sprigs.
Pair: Enjoy as a refreshing snack, post-workout drink, or breakfast boost.

Nutritional Info (Per Serving)

Calories: 140 | Protein: 2g | Carbs: 30g | Fats: 1g
Fiber: 4g | Cholesterol: 0mg | Sodium: 60mg | Potassium: 450mg
This Cucumber Mint Smoothie is hydrating, vibrant, and perfect for a warm day!

Chapter 3: Soups and Salads

Creamy Coconut Tomato Soup

Prep. time: 10 min   Cook time: 20 min   Serves: 4

Ingredients

Tomatoes (fresh or canned): 500g
Coconut milk: 1 cup (240ml)
Vegetable broth: 2 cups (480ml)
Onion (finely chopped): 1 medium
Garlic (minced): 3 cloves
Olive oil: 1 tbsp
Ground cumin: 1 tsp
Smoked paprika: 1 tsp
Turmeric powder: ½ tsp
Salt: 1 tsp (adjust to taste)
Black pepper: ½ tsp
Maple syrup: 1 tsp (optional)
Fresh basil or cilantro: 2 tbsp (chopped)
Pumpkin or sunflower seeds: 2 tbsp

Directions

Sauté Aromatics: Heat olive oil in a pot over medium heat. Add onions and garlic; sauté until translucent, about 3 minutes.
Add Spices: Stir in cumin, smoked paprika, and turmeric. Cook for 1 minute until fragrant.
Cook Tomatoes: Add chopped fresh tomatoes (or canned) and cook until softened, about 5 minutes.
Simmer Base: Pour in vegetable broth. Bring to a boil, reduce heat, and simmer for 10 minutes.
Blend: Use an immersion blender or transfer the mixture to a blender. Blend until smooth. Return to the pot.
Add Coconut Milk: Stir in coconut milk and maple syrup (if using). Heat gently, without boiling, for 3-5 minutes. Adjust seasoning with salt and pepper.
Serve: Ladle into bowls and garnish with fresh herbs, seeds, or desired toppings.

Nutritional Info (Per Serving):

Calories: 180 | Protein: 3g | Carbs: 16g | Fats: 13g
Fiber: 4g | Cholesterol: 0mg | Sodium: 600mg | Potassium: 550 mg

Hearty Lentil and Veggie Stew

Prep. time: 10 min   Cook time: 35 min   Serves: 4

Ingredients

Green or brown lentils (dry, rinsed): 1 cup (200g)
Vegetable broth: 4 cups (960ml)
Carrots (diced): 2 medium
Celery stalks (diced): 2 medium
Potatoes (cubed): 2 medium (300g)
Zucchini (diced): 1 medium
Onion (chopped): 1 medium
Garlic (minced): 3 cloves
Tomatoes (canned, diced): 1 cup (240ml)
Olive oil: 1 tbsp; Bay leaf: 1
Smoked paprika: 1 tsp
Ground cumin: 1 tsp
Thyme (dried): 1 tsp
Salt: 1 tsp (adjust to taste)
Black pepper: ½ tsp
Fresh parsley or cilantro: 2 tbsp (chopped)

Directions

Prep Ingredients: Rinse lentils and dice vegetables uniformly for even cooking.
Sauté Aromatics: Heat olive oil in a large pot over medium heat. Sauté onion and garlic until fragrant, about 3 minutes.
Add Spices: Stir in smoked paprika, cumin, thyme, and bay leaf; cook for 1 minute.
Add Veggies and Lentils: Add carrots, celery, potatoes, and lentils. Stir well to coat with spices.
Simmer: Pour in vegetable broth and canned tomatoes. Bring to a boil, then reduce heat to low. Cover and simmer for 25-30 minutes, stirring occasionally, until lentils and veggies are tender.
Adjust Seasoning: Remove bay leaf and adjust salt and pepper to taste.
Serve: Ladle into bowls and garnish with fresh parsley or cilantro.

Nutritional Info (Per Serving):

Calories: 220 | Protein: 12g | Carbs: 37g | Fats: 4g
Fiber: 10g | Cholesterol: 0mg | Sodium: 600mg | Potassium: 700mg

Thai-Inspired Peanut Noodle Salad

Prep. time: 15 min   Setting time: 15 min   Serves: 4

Ingredients

Rice noodles (or soba): 8 oz (225g)
Carrots (julienned): 2 medium
Red bell pepper (thinly sliced): 1 medium
Cucumber (thinly sliced): 1 small
Purple cabbage (shredded): 1 cup (80g)
Cilantro (chopped): 2 tbsp
Roasted peanuts (chopped): ¼ cup (30g)
Dressing:
Natural peanut butter: ¼ cup (60g)
Soy sauce (low sodium): 3 tbsp
Rice vinegar: 2 tbsp
Maple syrup: 1 tbsp
Lime juice: 2 tbsp
Garlic (minced): 2 cloves
Ginger (grated): 1 tsp
Water: 2-3 tbsp (to thin, if needed)

Directions

Cook Noodles: Cook noodles according to package instructions. Rinse under cold water and drain.

To prepare the Dressing, Whisk together peanut butter, soy sauce, rice vinegar, maple syrup, lime juice, garlic, ginger, and water until smooth.

Assemble Salad: In a large bowl, combine noodles, carrots, bell pepper, cucumber, and cabbage. Toss with dressing until well coated.

Garnish: Top with cilantro and chopped peanuts.

Chill: Let sit for 15 minutes for flavors to meld before serving.

Serving Suggestions:

Serve as a standalone meal or pair with miso soup for a light dinner.

Nutritional Info (Per Serving):

Calories: 320 | Protein: 9g | Carbs: 42g | Fats: 12g
Fiber: 5g | Cholesterol: 0mg | Sodium: 450mg | Potassium: 400mg

Fresh Kale and Quinoa Power Bowl

Prep. time: 10 min   Cook time: 20 min   Serves: 4

Ingredients

Quinoa 1 cup (185g), rinsed
Water or vegetable broth 2 cups (480ml)
Kale 4 cups (120g), chopped, stems removed.
Cherry tomatoes 1 cup (150g), halved.
Cucumber 1 medium, diced.
Avocado 1 medium, sliced
Chickpeas 1 cup (240g), cooked or canned, rinsed
Lemon juice three tablespoons, divided
Olive oil two tablespoons
Tahini 2 tablespoons
Maple syrup one teaspoon
Garlic 1 clove, minced
Salt ½ teaspoon
Black pepper ¼ teaspoon

Directions

Cook Quinoa: Cook quinoa in water or vegetable broth over medium heat for 15 minutes or until the liquid is absorbed. Fluff with a fork and let cool slightly.

Massage Kale: Massage chopped kale with one tablespoon of lemon juice and a pinch of salt for 2 to 3 minutes until softened.

Prepare the Dressing: In a small bowl, whisk together tahini, olive oil, two tablespoons of lemon juice, maple syrup, minced garlic, salt, and black pepper. Add water as needed to thin the dressing.

Assemble Bowl: Combine cooked quinoa, massaged kale, cherry tomatoes, cucumber, and chickpeas in a large bowl. Toss with the dressing until evenly coated.

Add Toppings: Top with sliced avocado and serve immediately.

Nutritional Info (Per Serving):

Calories: 320 | Protein: 11g | Carbs: 36g | Fats: 14g
Fiber: 8g | Cholesterol: 0mg | Sodium: 450mg | Potassium: 620mg

Comforting Butternut Squash Soup

Prep. time: 10 min   Cook time: 30 min   Serves: 4

Ingredients

Butternut squash one medium (about 2 lbs),
peeled, seeded, and cubed
Carrot 1 medium, chopped.
Onion 1 medium, diced.
Garlic 2 cloves, minced
Vegetable broth 4 cups (960ml)
Coconut milk 1 cup (240ml), unsweetened
Olive oil one tablespoon
Ground cinnamon ½ teaspoon
Ground nutmeg ¼ teaspoon
Salt 1 teaspoon
Black pepper ¼ teaspoon

Directions

Sauté Aromatics: Heat olive oil in a large pot over medium heat. Add onion, garlic, carrot, and sauté for 5 minutes until softened.
Cook Squash: Add cubed butternut squash to the pot. Sprinkle with cinnamon and nutmeg. Pour in vegetable broth and bring to a boil. Reduce heat, cover, and simmer for 20 minutes until the squash is tender.
Blend Soup: Remove the pot from heat and use an immersion blender to puree until smooth. Alternatively, transfer to a blender in batches and blend carefully.
Add Coconut Milk: Stir in coconut milk for creaminess. Season with salt and pepper, adjusting to taste. Reheat gently if needed.
Serving Suggestions:
Serve with crusty whole-grain bread or a side salad for a complete meal.

Nutritional Info (Per Serving):
Calories: 180 | Protein: 3g | Carbs: 22g | Fats: 8g
Fiber: 4g | Cholesterol: 0mg | Sodium: 600mg | Potassium: 580mg

Rainbow Chickpea Salad with Lemon Dressing

Prep. time: 15 min   Total time: 15 min   Serves: 4

Ingredients

Chickpeas 1 can (15 oz), rinsed and drained.
Red bell pepper, one medium, diced.
Yellow bell pepper, one medium, diced.
Cucumber 1 medium, diced.
Cherry tomatoes 1 cup, halved.
Red onion ¼ cup, finely chopped
Fresh parsley ¼ cup, chopped.
Lemon juice three tablespoons
Olive oil two tablespoons
Dijon mustard, one teaspoon
Maple syrup one teaspoon
Garlic 1 clove, minced
Salt ½ teaspoon
Black pepper ¼ teaspoon

Directions

Prepare Vegetables: Combine chickpeas, red and yellow bell peppers, cucumber, cherry tomatoes, red onion, and parsley in a large bowl.
Make Dressing: In a small bowl, whisk lemon juice, olive oil, Dijon mustard, maple syrup, minced garlic, salt, and black pepper until emulsified.
Combine Salad: Pour the dressing over the chickpea and vegetable mixture. Toss well to coat evenly.
Variations:
Add diced avocado for creaminess. Sprinkle with hemp hearts or sunflower seeds for a crunch. For a different flavor profile, use cilantro instead of parsley.
Serving Suggestions:
Serve as a light lunch or a side dish alongside whole-grain bread or soup.

Nutritional Info (Per Serving):
Calories: 200 | Protein: 6g | Carbs: 26g | Fats: 7g
Fiber: 7g | Cholesterol: 0mg | Sodium: 400mg | Potassium: 450mg

Smoky Black Bean and Corn Salad

Prep. time: 15 min   Total time: 15 min   Serves: 4

Ingredients

Black beans one can (15 oz), rinsed and drained.
Sweet corn 1 cup, cooked or canned and drained
Red bell pepper, one medium, diced.
Red onion ¼ cup, finely chopped
Cherry tomatoes 1 cup, halved.
Cilantro ¼ cup, chopped.
Olive oil two tablespoons
Lime juice three tablespoons
Smoked paprika, one teaspoon
Ground cumin ½ teaspoon
Garlic powder ½ teaspoon
Salt ½ teaspoon
Black pepper ¼ teaspoon

Directions

Prepare Vegetables: In a large bowl, combine black beans, corn, red bell pepper, red onion, cherry tomatoes, and cilantro.

To make the Dressing, Whisk the olive oil, lime juice, smoked paprika, cumin, garlic powder, salt, and black pepper in a small bowl until well combined.

Combine Salad: Pour the dressing over the black bean mixture. Toss gently to ensure everything is evenly coated.

Variations:

Add diced avocado for richness or roasted sweet potatoes for a hearty touch. Sprinkle with pumpkin seeds or a dash of hot sauce for extra flavor.

Serving Suggestions:

Serve as a vibrant side dish or a filling for tacos or burritos. Pair with tortilla chips for a fun snack.

Nutritional Info (Per Serving):

Calories: 190 | Protein: 7g | Carbs: 27g | Fats: 5g
Fiber: 7g | Cholesterol: 0mg | Sodium: 450mg | Potassium: 550mg

15-Minute Tomato Basil Gazpacho

Prep. time: 15 min   Total time: 15 min   Serves: 4

Ingredients

Ripe tomatoes four medium, roughly chopped
Cucumber 1 medium, peeled and diced.
Red bell pepper, one medium, diced.
Red onion ¼ cup, finely chopped
Garlic 1 clove, minced
Fresh basil ¼ cup, chopped.
Olive oil two tablespoons
Red wine vinegar, two tablespoons
Lemon juice one tablespoon
Salt ½ teaspoon
Black pepper ¼ teaspoon

Directions

Blend Vegetables: Combine tomatoes, cucumber, red bell pepper, red onion, and garlic in a blender. Blend until smooth.

Add Seasonings: Add olive oil, red wine vinegar, lemon juice, salt, and black pepper to the blender. Blend again until well combined.

Adjust Texture: For a chunkier texture, pulse the mixture briefly instead of blending until smooth.

Chill: To get the best flavor, transfer the gazpacho to the refrigerator and chill for at least 10 minutes before serving.

Serving Suggestions

Serve cold in bowls or glasses as a refreshing appetizer or light meal. For a heartier option, pair with crusty whole-grain bread.

Nutritional Info (Per Serving)

Calories: 120 | Protein: 2g | Carbs: 15g | Fats: 6g
Fiber: 3g | Cholesterol: 0mg | Sodium: 400mg | Potassium: 500mg

Crunchy Asian Slaw with Sesame Ginger Dressing

Prep. time: 15 min   Total time: 15 min   Serves: 4

Ingredients

Shredded red cabbage 2 cups
Shredded green cabbage 2 cups
Carrot 1 large, julienned
Red bell pepper one medium, thinly sliced
Edamame 1 cup, shelled
Green onion ¼ cup, sliced
Cilantro ¼ cup, chopped.
Sesame oil two tablespoons
Rice vinegar two tablespoons
Soy sauce or tamari one tablespoon
Maple syrup one teaspoon
Fresh ginger, one teaspoon, grated
Garlic 1 clove, minced
Lime juice one tablespoon
Toasted sesame seeds, one tablespoon

Directions

Prepare Vegetables: In a large mixing bowl, combine red cabbage, green cabbage, carrot, red bell pepper, edamame, green onion, and cilantro.

To make the Dressing, Whisk the sesame oil, rice vinegar, soy sauce, maple syrup, grated ginger, minced garlic, and lime juice in a small bowl until well blended.

Combine Salad: Pour the dressing over the vegetables and toss thoroughly to coat. Sprinkle with toasted sesame seeds before serving.

Variations

Add sliced avocado or crushed peanuts for extra creaminess and crunch. For variety, include spiralized zucchini or daikon radish.

Serving Suggestions

For a complete meal, serve as a side dish or top with baked tofu or tempeh. Enjoy alongside miso soup or rice.

Nutritional Info (Per Serving)

Calories: 180 | Protein: 6g | Carbs: 20g | Fats: 8g
Fiber: 5g | Cholesterol: 0mg | Sodium: 450mg | Potassium: 600mg

Creamy Avocado and Spinach Salad

Prep. time: 15 min   Total time: 15 min   Serves: 4

Ingredients

Baby spinach 4 cups
Ripe avocado, one large, sliced.
Cherry tomatoes 1 cup, halved.
Cucumber 1 medium, thinly sliced
Red onion ¼ cup, finely sliced
Pumpkin seeds two tablespoons
Olive oil two tablespoons
Lemon juice two tablespoons
Dijon mustard, one teaspoon
Maple syrup one teaspoon
Garlic 1 clove, minced
Salt ½ teaspoon
Black pepper ¼ teaspoon

Directions

Prepare Vegetables: In a large salad bowl, combine baby spinach, sliced avocado, cherry tomatoes, cucumber, red onion, and pumpkin seeds.

To make the Dressing, Whisk the olive oil, lemon juice, Dijon mustard, maple syrup, minced garlic, salt, and black pepper in a small bowl until smooth.

Combine Salad: Drizzle the dressing over the salad and toss gently to avoid mashing the avocado slices.

Variations

Add cooked quinoa or chickpeas for extra protein. Sprinkle with nutritional yeast for a cheesy flavor.

Serving Suggestions

Serve as a standalone light meal or pair with whole-grain bread or soup.

Nutritional Info (Per Serving)

Calories: 190 | Protein: 4g | Carbs: 13g | Fats: 14g
Fiber: 6g | Cholesterol: 0mg | Sodium: 300mg | Potassium: 700mg

Spiced Sweet Potato and Carrot Soup

Prep. time: 10 min   Total time: 30 min   Serves: 4

Ingredients

sweet potatoes (peeled and diced) 2 medium
carrots (peeled and chopped) 3 medium
onion (diced) 1
garlic (minced) 3 cloves
coconut oil 1 tbsp
ground cumin 1 tsp
ground turmeric 1/2 tsp
ground ginger 1/2 tsp
vegetable broth 4 cups
canned coconut milk (unsweetened) 1/2 cup
lime juice 1 tbsp
salt 1/2 tsp (or to taste)
black pepper 1/4 tsp
Optional Toppings
fresh cilantro
toasted pumpkin seeds
Drizzle of coconut milk

Directions

Sauté Vegetables: Heat the coconut oil in a large pot over medium heat. Add the onion, garlic, and sauté for 5-7 minutes until softening.
Add Spices: Stir in cumin, turmeric, and ginger. Cook for 1-2 minutes to release their fragrance.
Cook Vegetables: Add the diced sweet potatoes and carrots to the pot. Pour in the vegetable broth, boil, then reduce the heat to a simmer. Cover and cook for 20-25 minutes or until the vegetables are tender.
Blend Soup: Use an immersion blender to blend the soup until smooth, or transfer it to a blender in batches.
Finish Soup: Stir in coconut milk, lime juice, salt, and pepper. Taste and adjust seasoning as needed.
Serve: Ladle the soup into bowls and top with fresh cilantro, toasted pumpkin seeds, or a drizzle of coconut milk for extra creaminess.

Nutritional Info (Per Serving)

Calories: 200 | Protein: 3g | Carbs: 35g | Fats: 8g
Fiber: 6g | Cholesterol: 0mg | Sodium: 600mg | Potassium: 850mg

Mediterranean Orzo Salad with Fresh Herbs

Prep. time: 15 min   Cook time: 10 min   Serves: 4

Ingredients

orzo pasta 1 cup
cherry tomatoes (halved) 1 cup
cucumber (diced) 1 medium
red onion (thinly sliced) 1/4 medium
black olives (pitted and sliced) 1/4 cup
fresh parsley (chopped) 1/4 cup
fresh mint (chopped) 2 tbsp
lemon juice 2 tbsp
extra virgin olive oil 2 tbsp
garlic (minced) 1 clove
salt 1/2 tsp (or to taste)
black pepper 1/4 tsp
Optional Toppings
crumbled vegan feta
toasted pine nuts
avocado slices

Directions

Cook Orzo: Cook the orzo pasta according to the package instructions. Drain and rinse under cold water to stop the cooking process.
Combine Vegetables: In a large bowl, combine the cherry tomatoes, cucumber, red onion, and olives.
Add Herbs and Dressing: Add the cooked orzo to the vegetable mixture, followed by the chopped parsley and mint. Whisk together lemon juice, olive oil, garlic, salt, and black pepper in a small bowl.
Toss Salad: Pour the dressing over the salad and toss to combine, ensuring everything is well coated.
Serve: Divide the salad into bowls and top with optional toppings such as crumbled vegan feta, toasted pine nuts, or avocado slices.

Nutritional Info (Per Serving)

Calories: 250 | Protein: 5g | Carbs: 30g | Fats: 12g
Fiber: 4g | Cholesterol: 0mg | Sodium: 400mg | Potassium: 300mg
This Mediterranean Orzo Salad is a vibrant, refreshing, and nutrient-packed dish, perfect for a light lunch or as a side at any meal!

Rustic White Bean and Kale Soup

Prep. time: 10 min   Total time: 30 min   Serves: 4

Ingredients

canned white beans (drained and rinsed) 2 cups
fresh kale (chopped) 2 cups
carrot (diced) 1 medium
celery stalks (diced) 2
yellow onion (diced) 1 medium
garlic (minced) 3 cloves
vegetable broth 4 cups
extra virgin olive oil 1 tbsp
dried thyme 1 tsp
dried rosemary 1/2 tsp
bay leaf 1
salt 1/2 tsp (or to taste)
black pepper 1/4 tsp
lemon juice 1 tbsp (optional)
Optional Toppings
fresh parsley (chopped)
crusty bread for dipping

Directions

Sauté Vegetables: Heat olive oil over medium heat in a large pot. Add diced onion, carrot, celery, and sauté for 5-7 minutes until softened. Add garlic and cook for another 1-2 minutes until fragrant.

Add Broth and Beans: Add the vegetable broth, white beans, thyme, rosemary, bay leaf, salt, and black pepper to the pot. Stir to combine. Bring the mixture to a simmer and cook for 20 minutes to allow the flavors to meld.

Add Kale: Stir in the chopped kale and cook for 5 minutes until tender.

Finish Soup: Remove the bay leaf and add lemon juice, if using, for an added burst of flavor.

Serve: Ladle the soup into bowls and garnish with fresh parsley. If desired, serve with crusty bread for dipping.

Nutritional Info (Per Serving)

Calories: 220 | Protein: 10g | Carbs: 35g | Fats: 5g
Fiber: 9g | Cholesterol: 0mg | Sodium: 500mg | Potassium: 800mg
This hearty and wholesome soup is perfect for warming up on cool days. It offers a balanced protein, fiber, and nutrients to fuel your body deliciously and sustainably.

Zesty Citrus and Arugula Salad with Walnuts

Prep. time:10 min   Total time: 10 min   Serves: 4

Ingredients

arugula 4 cups
orange (peeled and segmented) 1 large
grapefruit (peeled and segmented) 1 medium
walnuts (toasted) 1/4 cup
avocado (sliced) 1
red onion (thinly sliced) 1/4 small
extra virgin olive oil 2 tbsp
fresh lemon juice 1 tbsp
Maple syrup 1 tsp (optional)
salt 1/4 tsp
black pepper 1/4 tsp
Optional Toppings
hemp seeds or chia seeds
crushed black pepper for extra zest

Directions

Prepare Salad: In a large bowl, combine the arugula, orange segments, grapefruit segments, sliced avocado, and red onion.

Toast Walnuts: In a small pan, toast the walnuts over medium heat for 3-4 minutes until fragrant and slightly golden. Remove from heat and let cool.

Make Dressing: In a small bowl, whisk together the olive oil, lemon juice, maple syrup (if using), salt, and black pepper until well combined.

Assemble Salad: Drizzle the dressing over the salad and toss gently to combine.

Top and Serve: Sprinkle toasted walnuts on top of the salad. Add optional toppings like hemp seeds or crushed black pepper for extra flavor and nutrients. Serve immediately.

Nutritional Info (Per Serving)

Calories: 220 | Protein: 4g | Carbs: 18g | Fats: 18g
Fiber: 6g | Cholesterol: 0mg | Sodium: 180mg | Potassium: 600mg

Chapter 4: Lunches on the Go

Crunchy Rainbow Veggie Spring Rolls with Peanut Sauce

Prep. time: 20 min   Total time: 20 min   Serves: 4

Ingredients

For the Spring Rolls:
rice paper wrappers, eight large
carrot (julienned) 1 medium
red bell pepper (thinly sliced) 1
cucumber (julienned) 1 medium
purple cabbage (shredded) 1 cup
avocado (sliced) 1
fresh cilantro or mint leaves 1/4 cup
For the Peanut Sauce:
natural peanut butter 1/4 cup
soy sauce or tamari 2 tbsp
lime juice 1 tbsp
Maple syrup 1 tbsp
water 2-3 tbsp (to thin)
minced garlic, one clove
grated ginger 1 tsp

Directions

Prepare Peanut Sauce: In a small bowl, whisk together peanut butter, soy sauce, lime juice, maple syrup, garlic, and ginger. Gradually add water to reach the desired consistency. Set aside.

Prep Veggies: Wash and thinly slice all vegetables. Arrange them on a plate or cutting board for easy assembly.

Soften Wrappers: Fill a large shallow dish with warm water. Submerge one rice paper wrapper for 10-15 seconds until soft but not overly pliable.

Assemble Rolls: Place the softened wrapper on a clean surface. Arrange a small amount of carrot, bell pepper, cucumber, cabbage, avocado, and herbs near the center of the wrapper. Fold the sides inward, then roll tightly from the bottom up. Repeat for all wrappers.

Serve: If desired, slice the rolls in half for presentation. Serve with the peanut sauce on the side for dipping.

Nutritional Info (Per Serving)

Calories: 190 | Protein: 5g | Carbs: 20g | Fats: 10g
Fiber: 4g | Cholesterol: 0mg | Sodium: 400mg | Potassium: 450mg

Creamy Avocado Chickpea Stuffed Pita

Prep. time: 10 min   Total time: 10 min   Serves: 2

Ingredients

For the Filling:
cooked chickpeas (rinsed and drained) 1 cup
ripe avocado (mashed) 1 medium
lemon juice 1 tbsp
olive oil 1 tbsp
minced garlic, one clove
ground cumin 1/2 tsp
salt and pepper to taste
For the Pita:
Whole wheat pita pockets 2
Baby spinach or arugula 1 cup
sliced cucumber 1/2 cup
grated carrot 1/4 cup
Optional Toppings:
sunflower seeds 1 tbsp
red pepper flakes 1/4 tsp

Directions

Mash Filling: In a bowl, mash chickpeas and avocado until slightly chunky. Stir in lemon juice, olive oil, garlic, cumin, salt, and pepper until combined.

Prepare Pita: Warm the pita pockets slightly to make them pliable. Slice each pita in half to form pockets.

Stuff Pita: Gently fill each pita half with a layer of baby spinach or arugula, followed by the creamy chickpea avocado. Add cucumber slices and grated carrot for crunch.

Add Toppings: Sprinkle sunflower seeds and red pepper flakes for added texture and flavor.

Serve: Serve immediately as a quick, satisfying meal or snack.

Nutritional Info (Per Serving)

Calories: 280 | Protein: 7g | Carbs: 30g | Fats: 14g
Fiber: 8g | Cholesterol: 0mg | Sodium: 420mg | Potassium: 600mg
This easy and delicious stuffed pita combines creamy and crunchy textures, bursting with fresh, wholesome ingredients perfect for a plant-based lifestyle.

Hearty Barbecue Jackfruit Sliders

Prep. time: 10 min   Cook time: 20 min   Serves: 4 (8 sliders)

Ingredients
For the Jackfruit:
canned young jackfruit (in water or brine, rinsed and drained) 2 cups
olive oil 1 tbsp
minced onion 1/4 cup
minced garlic, two cloves
smoked paprika 1 tsp
ground cumin 1/2 tsp
barbecue sauce (your choice) 1/2 cup
For the Sliders:
slider buns (whole grain or gluten-free) 8
vegan coleslaw 1 cup
sliced pickles 1/2 cup
Optional Toppings:
sliced red onion 1/4 cup
chopped fresh cilantro 2 tbsp

Directions
Repair jackfruit: Shred pieces with a fork or your hands to resemble pulled meat.
Cook Jackfruit: Heat olive oil in a skillet over medium heat. Add onion and garlic, and sauté until fragrant. Stir in shredded jackfruit, smoked paprika, and cumin. Sauté for 5 minutes.
Add Barbecue Sauce: Pour barbecue sauce into the skillet and mix to coat the jackfruit evenly. Simmer on low heat for 10 minutes, stirring occasionally.
Assemble Sliders: Lightly toast slider buns. Spread a layer of barbecue jackfruit on the bottom bun, and top with vegan coleslaw, pickles, and optional toppings like red onion or cilantro. Place the top bun on the sliders.
Serve: Serve warm with sweet potato fries or a crisp green salad.

Nutritional Info (Per Serving)
Calories: 190 | Protein: 4g | Carbs: 24g | Fats: 6g
Fiber: 5g | Cholesterol: 0mg | Sodium: 560mg | Potassium: 480mg

Zesty Lime and Cilantro Rice Burrito Bowls

Prep. time: 10 min   Cook time: 20 min   Serves: 4

Ingredients
For the Rice:
cooked brown rice 2 cups
lime juice 2 tbsp
lime zest 1 tsp
chopped fresh cilantro 1/4 cup
olive oil 1 tbsp
salt 1/2 tsp
For the Bowls:
black beans (rinsed and drained) 1 cup
diced tomatoes 1 cup
corn kernels (fresh or frozen) 1 cup
sliced avocado 1
shredded lettuce 1 cup
Optional Toppings:
salsa 1/2 cup
vegan sour cream 1/4 cup
sliced jalapeños 2 tbsp
crushed tortilla chips 1/4 cup

Directions
Prepare Rice: In a large bowl, mix warm cooked rice with lime juice, lime zest, cilantro, olive oil, and salt. Stir to combine and set aside.
Heat Beans and Corn: In a skillet over medium heat, warm black beans and corn until heated through.
Assemble Bowls: Divide lime-cilantro rice evenly into four bowls—layer with black beans, corn, diced tomatoes, shredded lettuce, and sliced avocado.
Add Toppings: Garnish each bowl with salsa, vegan sour cream, jalapeños, or crushed tortilla chips for added flavor and texture.
Serve: Serve immediately as a refreshing and hearty meal.

Nutritional Info (Per Serving)
Calories: 250 | Protein: 6g | Carbs: 36g | Fats: 9g
Fiber: 8g | Cholesterol: 0mg | Sodium: 480mg | Potassium: 680mg
These vibrant burrito bowls are packed with zesty flavors and plant-based goodness, making them perfect for quick and satisfying meals.

Mediterranean Hummus Wrap

Prep. time: 15 min   Total time: 15 min   Serves: 4

Ingredients

Large whole-grain tortillas 4
Hummus 1 cup
Cucumber 1 medium, thinly sliced
Cherry tomatoes 1 cup, halved.
Red onion ¼ cup, thinly sliced
Kalamata olives ¼ cup pitted and sliced.
Spinach or mixed greens 2 cups
Fresh parsley ¼ cup, chopped.
Lemon juice two tablespoons
Olive oil one tablespoon
Salt ¼ teaspoon
Black pepper ¼ teaspoon

Directions

Spread Hummus: Lay out the tortillas and spread a generous layer of hummus across the center.
Add Vegetables: Layer cucumber slices, cherry tomatoes, red onion, olives, spinach, and parsley evenly on each tortilla.
Season: Drizzle lemon juice and olive oil over the vegetables. Sprinkle with salt and black pepper.
Wrap: Fold the sides of each tortilla inward, then roll tightly into a wrap. Slice in half for easier serving.
Variations
Add roasted red peppers, artichoke hearts, or sun-dried tomatoes for extra Mediterranean flair. For a protein boost, add chickpeas or falafel.

Nutritional Info (Per Serving)

Calories: 220 | Protein: 6g | Carbs: 28g | Fats: 8g
Fiber: 5g | Cholesterol: 0mg | Sodium: 500mg | Potassium: 450mg

Roasted Veggie and Pesto Pasta Salad

Prep. time: 15 min   Cook time: 25 min   Serves: 4

Ingredients

Whole-grain pasta 2 cups, uncooked
Zucchini 1 medium, diced
Red bell pepper, one medium, diced.
Cherry tomatoes 1 cup, halved.
Red onion ½ medium, sliced
Olive oil two tablespoons
Salt ½ teaspoon
Black pepper ¼ teaspoon
Basil pesto (plant-based) ½ cup
Baby spinach 2 cups
Pine nuts two tablespoons, toasted (optional)

Directions

Cook Pasta: Cook pasta according to package instructions. Rinse under cold water and drain.
Roast Vegetables: Preheat oven to 400°F (200°C). Toss zucchini, red bell pepper, cherry tomatoes, and red onion with olive oil, salt, and pepper. Spread on a baking sheet and roast for 20 minutes, turning halfway.
Combine Salad: In a large bowl, mix cooked pasta, roasted vegetables, spinach, and pesto until well coated.
Serve: Top with toasted pine nuts, if desired, and serve warm or chilled.
Variations
Add roasted asparagus or mushrooms for more variety. Use gluten-free pasta for a gluten-free option.
Serving Suggestions
Serve as a main dish alongside a fresh green salad and crusty whole-grain bread.

Nutritional Info (Per Serving)

Calories: 260 | Protein: 7g | Carbs: 35g | Fats: 9g
Fiber: 6g | Cholesterol: 0mg | Sodium: 450mg | Potassium: 650mg

Protein-packed Mason Jar Salads

Prep. time: 20 min   Total time: 20 min   Serves: 4

Ingredients

Cooked quinoa 1 cup
Cooked chickpeas 1 cup
Cherry tomatoes 1 cup, halved.
Cucumber 1 medium, diced.
Carrot 1 medium, shredded
Baby spinach 2 cups, chopped.
Red cabbage 1 cup, shredded.
Avocado 1 medium, diced (add before serving)
Lemon-tahini dressing ½ cup

Directions

Layer Ingredients: Layer the salad in four mason jars, starting with quinoa, then chickpeas, tomatoes, cucumber, carrot, cabbage, and spinach.
Add Dressing: Pour two tablespoons of lemon-tahini dressing into the bottom of each jar before layering, or keep it in a separate container to add before eating.
Store: Seal the jars tightly and refrigerate for up to 4 days.
Serve: Before eating, shake the jar to distribute the dressing or transfer it to a bowl. Add avocado just before serving to keep it fresh.

Variations
Add roasted sweet potatoes or edamame for extra flavor and protein. For a heartier option, use kale instead of spinach.

Serving Suggestions
Pair with whole-grain bread or a cup of soup for a complete meal.

Nutritional Info (Per Serving)
Calories: 320 | Protein: 10g | Carbs: 37g | Fats: 13g
Fiber: 9g | Cholesterol: 0mg | Sodium: 400mg | Potassium: 750mg

Easy Chickpea Salad Sandwich

Prep. time: 15 min   Total time: 15 min   Serves: 4

Ingredients

Cooked chickpeas 1½ cups, mashed
Celery 1 stalk, diced
Red onion ¼ cup, finely chopped
Dill pickle two tablespoons, chopped
Vegan mayonnaise three tablespoons
Dijon mustard, one teaspoon
Lemon juice one tablespoon
Salt and pepper to taste
Whole-grain bread, eight slices
Lettuce leaves 4
Tomato 1, sliced

Directions

Mash Chickpeas: Mash chickpeas in a bowl using a fork, leaving some chunks for texture.
Combine Ingredients: Mix mashed chickpeas with celery, red onion, dill pickle, vegan mayonnaise, Dijon mustard, lemon juice, salt, and pepper until well combined.
Assemble Sandwich: Place lettuce and tomato slices on one slice of bread. Spread the chickpea mixture evenly on the other slice of bread, then top with the remaining sandwich. Repeat for the remaining sandwiches.
Serve: Slice sandwiches in half and serve immediately, or wrap them for later.

Variations
Add shredded carrots or chopped bell peppers for extra crunch, and use sourdough or pita instead of bread.

Nutritional Info (Per Serving)
Calories: 260 | Protein: 8g | Carbs: 37g | Fats: 9g
Fiber: 7g | Cholesterol: 0mg | Sodium: 580mg | Potassium: 400mg

Spicy Soba Noodle Bento Box

Prep. time: 20 min   Total time: 20 min   Serves: 2

Ingredients

Soba noodles 4 ounces
Soy sauce two tablespoons
Sesame oil one teaspoon
Rice vinegar one tablespoon
Sriracha sauce one teaspoon
Garlic 1 clove, minced
Carrot 1, julienned
Cucumber ½, thinly sliced
Edamame ½ cup, cooked
Avocado 1, sliced
Sesame seeds one teaspoon
Fresh cilantro two tablespoons, chopped

Directions

Cook Noodles: Cook soba noodles according to package instructions. Rinse under cold water and drain.
Make Dressing: In a small bowl, whisk together soy sauce, sesame oil, rice vinegar, sriracha, and minced garlic.
Toss Noodles: In a large bowl, toss the cooled soba noodles with the spicy dressing until evenly coated.
Assemble Bento Box: Divide noodles between two bento boxes. Arrange carrot, cucumber, edamame, and avocado in separate sections.
Top and Garnish: Sprinkle sesame seeds and fresh cilantro on top of the noodles.
Serve: Pack the bento boxes and serve chilled or at room temperature.
Serving Suggestions
Serve with a side of fruit or miso soup for a complete meal.
Variations
Add pickled ginger or roasted seaweed for extra flavor. Use tempeh or tofu for additional protein.

Nutritional Info (Per Serving)
Calories: 380 | Protein: 15g | Carbs: 45g | Fats: 18g
Fiber: 8g | Cholesterol: 0mg | Sodium: 700mg | Potassium: 600mg

Vegan Caesar Salad Wrap

Prep. time: 15 min   Total time: 15 min   Serves: 2

Ingredients

Large flour tortillas 2
Romaine lettuce 3 cups, chopped
Chickpeas 1/2 cup, cooked or canned, drained
Vegan Caesar dressing 1/4 cup (store-bought or homemade)
Vegan parmesan cheese two tablespoons
Whole wheat croutons 1/4 cup
Lemon juice one tablespoon
Garlic powder 1/2 teaspoon
Black pepper to taste

Directions

Prepare the Lettuce: Wash and chop the romaine lettuce into bite-sized pieces.
Make the Dressing: In a small bowl, mix the vegan Caesar dressing with lemon juice, garlic powder, and black pepper.
Assemble the Salad: In a large bowl, toss the chopped lettuce, chickpeas, croutons, and vegan parmesan cheese with the Caesar dressing until evenly coated.
Prepare the Wrap: Lay the tortilla flat on a clean surface. Spoon the Caesar salad mixture into the center of each tortilla.
Wrap and Serve: Fold in the sides of the tortilla, then roll it up tightly into a wrap. Cut in half and serve immediately.

Serving Suggestions
Serve with baked sweet potato fries or a light fruit salad.

Nutritional Info (Per Serving)
Calories: 350 | Protein: 10g | Carbs: 40g | Fats: 15g
Fiber: 8g | Cholesterol: 0mg | Sodium: 500mg | Potassium: 700mg

Sweet Potato and Black Bean Tacos

Prep. time: 15 min   Setting time: 20 min   Serves: 4

Ingredients

Sweet potatoes are two medium, peeled, and diced.
Black beans one can (15 oz), drained and rinsed.
Olive oil one tablespoon
Taco seasoning one tablespoon (or to taste)
Corn tortillas, eight small
Avocado 1, sliced
Lime 1, cut into wedges.
Cilantro 1/4 cup, chopped.
Red onion 1/4 cup, finely chopped (optional)
Salsa 1/4 cup (optional)

Directions

Cook Sweet Potatoes: Preheat the oven to 400°F (200°C). Toss the diced sweet potatoes with olive oil and taco seasoning. Spread them on a baking sheet and roast for 20 minutes or until tender, flipping halfway through.

Prepare the Black Beans: While the sweet potatoes are roasting, warm the black beans in a small pot over low heat for 5 minutes, stirring occasionally.

Warm the Tortillas: Heat the corn tortillas in a dry skillet over medium heat for 30 seconds on each side or until warm and slightly charred.

Assemble the Tacos: Once the sweet potatoes are done, assemble the tacos by adding a few spoonfuls of roasted sweet potatoes and black beans to each tortilla.

Add Toppings: Top each taco with avocado slices, chopped cilantro, red onion (if using), and a squeeze of lime juice. Optionally, add salsa for extra flavor.

Nutritional Info (Per Serving)

Calories: 330 | Protein: 8g | Carbs: 50g | Fats: 13g
Fiber: 12g | Cholesterol: 0mg | Sodium: 450mg | Potassium: 750mg

Grilled Veggie and Quinoa Buddha Bowl

Prep. time: 15 min   Cook time: 25 min   Serves: 4
                            Setting time: 5 min

Ingredients

Quinoa 1 cup (uncooked)
Zucchini 1, sliced
Bell pepper 1, sliced
Red onion 1/2, sliced
Cherry tomatoes 1 cup, halved.
Olive oil two tablespoons
Lemon 1, juiced
Tahini 2 tablespoons
Garlic 1 clove, minced
Salt and pepper to taste
Fresh parsley 1/4 cup, chopped.
Optional Toppings: Avocado, hummus, sesame seeds, or pumpkin seeds

Directions

Cook Quinoa: Rinse the quinoa under cold water. Add the quinoa and 2 cups of water to a medium pot. Bring to a boil, then cover and simmer for about 15 minutes or until the water is absorbed. Remove from heat and fluff with a fork.

Grill the Vegetables: Preheat a grill or grill pan over medium heat. Toss the zucchini, bell pepper, red onion, and cherry tomatoes with one tablespoon of olive oil, salt, and pepper. Grill for 5-7 minutes until tender and slightly charred, turning occasionally.

Prepare Dressing: In a small bowl, whisk together tahini, lemon juice, minced garlic, and one tablespoon of olive oil. Add water and a teaspoon until you reach a creamy, pourable consistency—season with salt and pepper.

Assemble the Bowl: Add a serving of quinoa as the base in each bowl. Arrange the grilled veggies on top. Drizzle with the tahini dressing and garnish with chopped parsley.

Add Optional Toppings: For extra flavor and nutrition, top with sliced avocado, a dollop of hummus, or a sprinkle of sesame or pumpkin seeds.

Nutritional Info (Per Serving)

Calories: 350 | Protein: 10g | Carbs: 45g | Fats: 15g
Fiber: 7g | Cholesterol: 0mg | Sodium: 230mg | Potassium: 850mg

Italian-Inspired Marinated Tempeh Wrap

Prep. time: 10 min   Cook time: 10 min   Serves: 4
                            Setting time: 30 min

Ingredients

Tempeh 1 block (8 oz)
Olive oil two tablespoons
Balsamic vinegar two tablespoons
Dijon mustard, one teaspoon
Garlic powder 1/2 teaspoon
Dried oregano one teaspoon
Salt 1/4 teaspoon
Black pepper 1/4 teaspoon
Whole wheat wraps 4
Roma tomatoes 2, sliced
Fresh basil leaves 1/4 cup.
Mixed greens 2 cups
Hummus 1/4 cup
Lemon juice one tablespoon

Directions

Prepare Tempeh: Slice the tempeh into thin strips or small cubes.

Marinate Tempeh: In a small bowl, whisk together olive oil, balsamic vinegar, Dijon mustard, garlic powder, dried oregano, salt, and pepper. Place the tempeh in a shallow dish and pour the marinade over it. Toss to coat, then marinate for at least 30 minutes or longer for more flavor.

Cook Tempeh: Heat a non-stick pan over medium heat. Once hot, add the marinated tempeh and cook for 5-7 minutes, turning occasionally, until golden and slightly crispy.

Assemble Wrap: Spread a thin layer of hummus on each whole wheat wrap, then layer with mixed greens, tomato slices, cooked tempeh, and fresh basil leaves. Drizzle with lemon juice.

Wrap and Serve: Roll each wrap tightly, folding in the edges. Slice in half and serve.

Nutritional Info (Per Serving)

Calories: 320 | Protein: 16g | Carbs: 28g | Fats: 18g
Fiber: 7g | Cholesterol: 0mg | Sodium: 550mg | Potassium: 500mg

Quick Curry Lentil Rice Bowls

Prep. time: 10 min   Cook time: 25 min   Serves: 4

Ingredients

Brown rice 1 cup (uncooked)
Red lentils 1 cup (rinsed)
Olive oil one tablespoon
Onion 1 medium, diced.
Garlic 2 cloves, minced
Curry powder one tablespoon
Ground turmeric 1/2 teaspoon
Ground cumin 1/2 teaspoon
Coconut milk one can (14 oz)
Vegetable broth 1 cup
Spinach 2 cups, fresh
Lemon juice one tablespoon
Salt 1/2 teaspoon
Black pepper 1/4 teaspoon

Directions

Cook Rice: Cook the brown rice according to package instructions. Set aside.

Add the rinsed lentils and vegetable broth to a medium saucepan. Bring to a boil, then reduce heat and simmer for about 15 minutes until lentils are tender.

Cook Aromatics: Heat olive oil in a large pan over medium heat while cooking rice and lentils. Add the diced onion and cook for 3-4 minutes, until softened. Add the minced garlic and cook for another 1 minute.

Make curry sauce by stirring in curry powder, turmeric, and cumin. Then add the coconut milk, cooked lentils, salt, and pepper. Simmer for 5-7 minutes until the sauce thickens slightly.

Add Spinach: Stir in the fresh spinach and cook for 2 minutes until wilted.

Assemble Bowls: Divide the cooked rice among four bowls. Top each bowl with the curry lentil mixture. Drizzle with lemon juice for a fresh finish.

Serving Suggestions

Serve with a side of sliced cucumber or a dollop of plant-based yogurt.

Nutritional Info (Per Serving)

Calories: 350 | Protein: 14g | Carbs: 58g | Fats: 11g
Fiber: 10g | Cholesterol: 0mg | Sodium: 600mg | Potassium: 700mg

Chapter 5: Simple and Flavorful Dinners

Smoky Eggplant and Chickpea Stew

Prep. time: 10 min   Total time: 30 min   Serves: 4

Ingredients

olive oil 2 tbsp
diced onion 1
minced garlic, three cloves
eggplant (diced into 1-inch cubes) 2 cups
smoked paprika 2 tsp
ground cumin 1 tsp
crushed red pepper flakes (optional) 1/2 tsp
canned chickpeas (rinsed and drained) 1.5 cups
crushed tomatoes 1 cup
vegetable broth 1 cup
salt 1 tsp
black pepper 1/2 tsp
Optional Toppings:
fresh parsley (chopped) 2 tbsp
lemon wedges for serving

Directions

Sauté Aromatics: Heat olive oil in a large pot over medium heat. Add diced onion and minced garlic. Cook until softened, about 3 minutes.
Cook Eggplant: Add the eggplant to the pot and sauté until tender and slightly browned, about 7-8 minutes.
Season: Stir in smoked paprika, ground cumin, and crushed red pepper flakes. Cook for 1 minute to toast the spices.
Simmer Stew: Add chickpeas, crushed tomatoes, and vegetable broth—season with salt and black pepper. Stir well and bring to a boil.
Reduce Heat and Simmer: Lower the heat to medium-low, cover, and let simmer for 20 minutes, stirring occasionally, until the flavors meld and the stew thickens.
Serve: Ladle the stew into bowls. Garnish with fresh parsley and serve with lemon wedges for a zesty kick.

Nutritional Info (Per Serving)

Calories: 220 | Protein: 6g | Carbs: 24g | Fats: 10g
Fiber: 7g | Cholesterol: 0mg | Sodium: 600mg | Potassium: 580mg

One-Pot Garlic and Herb Orzo with Vegetables

Prep. time: 10 min   Cook time: 20 min   Serves: 4

Ingredients

olive oil 2 tbsp
minced garlic, four cloves
diced onion, one small
dry orzo 1 cup
vegetable broth 2 cups
zucchini (diced) 1 cup
cherry tomatoes (halved) 1 cup
Baby spinach 2 cups
dried oregano 1 tsp
dried thyme 1 tsp
salt 1 tsp
black pepper 1/2 tsp
lemon juice 2 tbsp
Optional Toppings:
fresh parsley (chopped) 2 tbsp
toasted pine nuts 2 tbsp

Directions

Sauté Aromatics: Heat olive oil in a large pot over medium heat. Add minced garlic and diced onion. Cook until fragrant and softened, about 3 minutes.
Toast Orzo: Add the dry orzo to the pot and sauté for 2 minutes, stirring frequently, until lightly golden.
Add Broth and Vegetables: Stir in vegetable broth, zucchini, cherry tomatoes, oregano, thyme, salt, and black pepper. Bring to a boil.
Simmer: Reduce heat to medium-low and cover. Cook for 10-12 minutes, stirring occasionally, until the orzo is tender and the liquid is mostly absorbed.
Add Spinach: Stir in baby spinach and cook for 2 minutes, until wilted.
Finish: Remove from heat and stir in lemon juice for brightness.
Serve: Ladle into bowls and garnish with fresh parsley and toasted pine nuts, if desired.

Nutritional Info (Per Serving)

Calories: 240 | Protein: 6g | Carbs: 30g | Fats: 10g
Fiber: 5g | Cholesterol: 0mg | Sodium: 580mg | Potassium: 620mg

Spicy Coconut Lentil Curry

Prep. time: 10 min   Cook time: 25 min   Serves: 4

Ingredients

red lentils (rinsed) 1 cup
coconut milk one can (13.5 oz)
vegetable broth 2 cups
diced tomatoes (canned or fresh) 1 cup
onion (diced) 1 medium
minced garlic, three cloves
grated ginger 1 tbsp
olive oil 1 tbsp
curry powder 2 tsp
ground cumin 1 tsp
turmeric 1/2 tsp
Red chili flakes 1/2 tsp (adjust for spice level)
salt 1 tsp
lime juice 1 tbsp
Optional Toppings:
fresh cilantro (chopped) 2 tbsp
toasted coconut flakes 2 tbsp

Directions

Sauté Aromatics: Heat olive oil in a large pot over medium heat. Add diced onion, garlic, and grated ginger. Sauté for 3-4 minutes until fragrant.

Toast Spices: Stir in curry powder, cumin, turmeric, and red chili flakes. Cook for 1 minute to enhance the spices' aroma.

Add Base Ingredients: Add lentils, coconut milk, vegetable broth, and diced tomatoes. Stir well and bring to a gentle boil.

Simmer: Reduce heat to low, cover, and simmer for 20 minutes, stirring occasionally, until the lentils are tender and the curry has thickened.

Season and Finish: Stir in lime juice and salt. Adjust seasoning as needed.

Serve: Ladle into bowls and garnish with fresh cilantro and toasted coconut flakes.

Nutritional Info (Per Serving)

Calories: 250 | Protein: 9g | Carbs: 28g | Fats: 11g
Fiber: 7g | Cholesterol: 0mg | Sodium: 620mg | Potassium: 650mg
This curry pairs beautifully with steamed rice, quinoa, or warm flatbread. For added crunch, serve with cucumber salad on the side.

Balsamic Glazed Roasted Veggie and Quinoa Bowl

Prep. time: 10 min   Cook time: 20 min   Serves: 4

Ingredients

quinoa (rinsed) 1 cup
vegetable broth 2 cups
cherry tomatoes (halved) 1 cup
zucchini (sliced) 1 medium
red bell pepper (diced) 1
red onion (sliced) 1 small
balsamic vinegar 3 tbsp
olive oil 2 tbsp
garlic powder 1 tsp
dried thyme 1/2 tsp
salt 1 tsp
pepper 1/2 tsp
Optional Toppings:
Baby spinach 1 cup
sliced avocado 1
toasted sunflower seeds 2 tbsp

Directions

Cook Quinoa: Bring vegetable broth to a boil in a medium pot. Add rinsed quinoa, reduce heat to low, cover, and simmer for 15 minutes. Remove from heat and let it sit for 5 minutes before fluffing with a fork.

Prepare Vegetables: Preheat oven to 400°F (200°C). Arrange cherry tomatoes, zucchini, bell pepper, and onion on a baking sheet. Drizzle with olive oil and balsamic vinegar. Sprinkle with garlic powder, thyme, salt, and pepper. Toss to coat evenly.

Roast Vegetables: Roast in the oven for 20-25 minutes, flipping halfway through, until vegetables are tender and slightly caramelized.

Assemble Bowls: Divide quinoa into bowls. Top with roasted vegetables and optional toppings like baby spinach, avocado slices, or sunflower seeds.

Serve: Drizzle additional balsamic vinegar or olive oil over the bowl for extra flavor if desired.

Nutritional Info (Per Serving)

Calories: 280 | Protein: 7g | Carbs: 34g | Fats: 11g
Fiber: 5g | Cholesterol: 0mg | Sodium: 580mg | Potassium: 650mg

Creamy Vegan Mushroom Stroganoff

Prep. time: 10 min   Cook time: 20 min   Serves: 4

Ingredients

wide noodles 8 oz (use gluten-free if desired)
olive oil 2 tbsp
Yellow onion, one medium-diced
garlic three cloves, minced
cremini or button mushrooms 16 oz, sliced
vegetable broth 1 cup
Unsweetened cashew cream 1 cup (blend 1/2 cup
soaked cashews with 3/4 cup water until smooth)
soy sauce or tamari 2 tbsp
nutritional yeast 2 tbsp
smoked paprika 1/2 tsp
cornstarch 1 tbsp mixed with 2 tbsp water
fresh parsley chopped for garnish
Optional Toppings or Variations
toasted pine nuts for added crunch
lemon zest for brightness
spinach or kale for added greens

Directions

Cook Noodles: Cook noodles according to package instructions. Rinse under cold water and drain.
Sauté Vegetables: Heat olive oil in a large skillet over medium heat. Add the onion and cook until translucent, about 3 minutes. Stir in garlic and cook for 1 minute. Add mushrooms and sauté until browned and softened, about 5-7 minutes.
Make Sauce: Pour vegetable broth into the skillet and simmer. Stir in cashew cream, soy sauce, nutritional yeast, and smoked paprika. Mix well and let the flavors meld for 2-3 minutes.
Thicken Sauce: Slowly stir in the cornstarch slurry. Continue cooking for 2 minutes until the sauce thickens. Adjust seasoning with salt and pepper if needed.
Combine Noodles and Sauce: Add the cooked noodles to the skillet and toss gently to coat them in the creamy sauce. Cook for 1-2 minutes to ensure everything is heated through.
Serve: Garnish with fresh parsley and any desired toppings. Serve immediately.

Nutritional Info (Per Serving)

Calories: 180 | Protein: 3g | Carbs: 16g | Fats: 13g
Fiber: 4g | Cholesterol: 0mg | Sodium: 600mg | Potassium: 550mg

Sheet Pan Roasted Veggie Medley

Prep. time: 10 min   Cook time: 30 min   Serves: 4

Ingredients

carrots two medium, sliced into sticks
sweet potatoes two medium, cubed
brussels sprouts 2 cups, halved
red bell pepper, one large, sliced
Red onion one large, cut into wedges.
olive oil 3 tbsp
garlic powder 1 tsp
paprika 1 tsp
dried thyme 1 tsp
sea salt 1/2 tsp
black pepper 1/4 tsp
Optional Toppings or Variations
toasted sesame seeds for crunch
balsamic glaze for sweetness
fresh herbs such as parsley or cilantro for added flavor

Directions

Preheat Oven: Preheat the oven to 425°F (220°C) and line a large sheet pan with parchment paper.
Prepare Veggies: Wash and chop the vegetables into uniform sizes to ensure even roasting.
Season Veggies: Place the prepared vegetables in a large bowl. Drizzle with olive oil and sprinkle with garlic powder, paprika, thyme, salt, and pepper. Toss well to coat evenly.
Roast Veggies: Spread the seasoned vegetables evenly on the sheet pan, ensuring they do not overlap too much. Roast in the preheated oven for 25-30 minutes, flipping halfway through, until the vegetables are golden and tender.
Serve: Transfer the roasted veggies to a serving platter. Add any desired toppings and serve immediately.

Nutritional Info (Per Serving)

Calories: 180 | Protein: 3g | Carbs: 16g | Fats: 13g
Fiber: 4g | Cholesterol: 0mg | Sodium: 600mg | Potassium: 550mg

Hearty Black Bean and Sweet Potato Chili

Prep. time: 10 min   Cook time: 30 min   Serves: 4

Ingredients

olive oil 2 tbsp
yellow onion, one medium diced
garlic three cloves, minced
sweet potatoes two medium, peeled and cubed
red bell pepper, one large, diced
black beans 2 cups, cooked (or one can, rinsed and drained)
diced tomatoes one can (14 oz) with juices
vegetable broth 2 cups
chili powder 1 tbsp
ground cumin 1 tsp
smoked paprika 1 tsp
cayenne pepper 1/4 tsp (optional)
sea salt 1/2 tsp
black pepper 1/4 tsp
Optional Toppings or Variations
diced avocado for creaminess
chopped cilantro for freshness
sliced jalapeños for heat
lime wedges for zest

Directions

Sauté Aromatics: Heat olive oil in a large pot over medium heat. Add onion and cook until soft, about 3 minutes. Stir in garlic and cook for 1 minute until fragrant.
Cook Vegetables: Add sweet potatoes and red bell pepper. Cook for 5 minutes, stirring occasionally.
Build the Chili Base: Stir in black beans, diced tomatoes with juices, and vegetable broth. Add chili powder, cumin, smoked paprika, cayenne, salt, and black pepper. Mix well to combine.
Simmer: Bring the mixture to a boil, then reduce the heat to low. Cover and simmer for 20-25 minutes or until the sweet potatoes are tender. Stir occasionally to prevent sticking.
Adjust Seasoning: Taste and adjust seasoning as needed.
Serve: Ladle the chili into bowls and add desired toppings. Serve warm with cornbread or over rice for a heartier meal.

Nutritional Info (Per Serving)

Calories: 180 | Protein: 6g | Carbs: 30g | Fats: 5g
Fiber: 8g | Cholesterol: 0mg | Sodium: 450mg | Potassium: 700mg

Zucchini Noodles with Pesto and Cherry Tomatoes

Prep. time: 10 min   Cook time: 5 min   Serves: 4

Ingredients

zucchini four medium, spiralized
Cherry tomatoes 2 cups, halved.
Basil leaves 2 cups, fresh and packed.
raw cashews 1/3 cup (soaked in warm water for 15 minutes, then drained)
nutritional yeast 2 tbsp
garlic two cloves
lemon juice 2 tbsp, fresh
olive oil 3 tbsp
sea salt 1/2 tsp
black pepper 1/4 tsp
Optional Toppings or Variations
toasted pine nuts for crunch
red pepper flakes for heat
vegan parmesan for extra cheesiness

Directions

Prepare Pesto: In a blender or food processor, combine basil leaves, soaked cashews, nutritional yeast, garlic, lemon juice, olive oil, salt, and pepper. Blend until smooth, adding 1-2 tablespoons of water for desired consistency.
Cook Zucchini Noodles: Heat a non-stick skillet over medium heat. Add the spiralized zucchini and sauté for 2-3 minutes until slightly tender but not soggy.
Combine: Remove the skillet from heat. Toss the zucchini noodles with the prepared pesto until evenly coated.
Add Tomatoes: Gently fold in the cherry tomatoes for freshness and color.
Serve: Transfer to bowls and garnish with optional toppings. Serve immediately.

Nutritional Info (Per Serving)

Calories: 180 | Protein: 4g | Carbs: 13g | Fats: 13g
Fiber: 3g | Cholesterol: 0mg | Sodium: 250mg | Potassium: 600mg

Thai Green Curry with Tofu and Veggies

Prep. time: 10 min   Cook time: 20 min   Serves: 4

Ingredients

firm tofu one block (14 oz), pressed and cubed
coconut oil 1 tbsp
Green curry paste 3 tbsp (ensure vegan)
coconut milk one can (13.5 oz)
vegetable broth 1 cup
broccoli florets 2 cups
red bell pepper, one large, sliced
carrot 1 large, julienned
zucchini one medium-sliced
Baby spinach 2 cups
lime juice 2 tbsp, fresh
soy sauce or tamari 1 tbsp
fresh basil leaves 1/4 cup
Optional Toppings or Variations
crushed peanuts for crunch
sliced red chilies for heat
cooked jasmine rice or rice noodles for serving

Directions

Prepare Tofu: Press the tofu to remove excess water, then cube it. Sauté in coconut oil over medium heat in a large pan until golden on all sides. Remove and set aside.

Cook Curry Base: In the same pan, add the green curry paste and sauté for 1 minute until fragrant. Stir in coconut milk and vegetable broth. Bring to a simmer.

Cook Vegetables: Add broccoli, bell pepper, carrot, and zucchini to the curry. Simmer for 8-10 minutes until vegetables are tender but not overcooked.

Combine: Stir in baby spinach, lime juice, soy sauce, and cooked tofu. Cook for an additional 2 minutes until spinach wilts.

Serve: Garnish with fresh basil leaves and optional toppings. Serve hot with jasmine rice or rice noodles.

Serving Suggestions

Pair with pickled vegetables or a simple cucumber salad for added freshness.

Nutritional Info (Per Serving)

Calories: 180 | Protein: 6g | Carbs: 14g | Fats: 12g
Fiber: 4g | Cholesterol: 0mg | Sodium: 500mg | Potassium: 700mg

Plant-Based Shepherd's Pie

Prep. time: 15 min   Cook time: 30 min   Serves: 4

Ingredients

russet potatoes, four medium peeled and cubed
unsweetened plant-based milk 1/3 cup
olive oil 2 tbsp
Yellow onion, one medium-diced
Carrot 2 medium, diced.
celery two stalks, diced
frozen peas 1 cup
lentils 1 1/2 cups, cooked (or one can, rinsed and drained)
tomato paste 2 tbsp
vegetable broth 1 cup
soy sauce 1 tbsp
dried thyme 1 tsp
paprika 1/2 tsp
sea salt 1/2 tsp
black pepper 1/4 tsp

Directions

Prepare Mashed Potatoes: Boil cubed potatoes in salted water for 12-15 minutes until tender. Drain and mash with plant-based milk, one tablespoon of olive oil, salt, and pepper. Set aside.

Cook Filling: Heat one tablespoon of olive oil in a skillet over medium heat. Sauté onion, carrot, and celery for 5-7 minutes until softened. Stir in tomato paste, lentils, vegetable broth, soy sauce, thyme, paprika, salt, and pepper. Simmer for 5 minutes until the mixture thickens slightly. Stir in peas and remove from heat.

Assemble: Preheat the oven to 375°F (190°C). Spread the filling evenly in a baking dish. Top with mashed potatoes, spreading them smoothly. Optionally, use a fork to create ridges on the surface.

Bake: In the oven for 15-20 minutes or until the top is slightly golden and bubbling.

Serve: Let cool for a few minutes before serving. Garnish with parsley or nutritional yeast if desired.

Nutritional Info (Per Serving)

Calories: 180 | Protein: 6g | Carbs: 25g | Fats: 5g
Fiber: 5g | Cholesterol: 0mg | Sodium: 450mg | Potassium: 700mg

30-Minute Veggie Stir-Fry with Sesame Sauce

Prep. time: 10 min   Cook time: 20 min   Serves: 4

Ingredients
broccoli florets 2 cups
red bell pepper, one large, sliced
carrot 1 large, julienned
Snap peas 1 cup
mushrooms 1 cup, sliced
green onion, two stalks, sliced
cooked rice or noodles 2 cups
For the Sesame Sauce
tamari or soy sauce 1/4 cup
sesame oil 1 tbsp
rice vinegar 1 tbsp
Maple syrup 1 tbsp
garlic two cloves, minced
ginger 1 tsp, grated
cornstarch 1 tsp mixed with 2 tbsp water

Directions
Make Sauce: In a small bowl, whisk together tamari, sesame oil, rice vinegar, maple syrup, garlic, ginger, and cornstarch slurry. Set aside.
Cook Vegetables: Heat a large skillet or wok over medium-high heat. Add a splash of water or a small amount of sesame oil. Stir-fry broccoli, bell pepper, carrot, snap peas, and mushrooms for 5-7 minutes until tender but crisp.
Add Sauce: Pour the sesame sauce into the skillet with the vegetables. Stir well to coat and cook for 2-3 minutes, thickening the sauce.
Combine: Stir in green onion and serve the stir-fry over cooked rice or noodles.
Serve: Garnish with sesame seeds and any additional toppings. Serve immediately.

Nutritional Info (Per Serving)
Calories: 180 | Protein: 5g | Carbs: 20g | Fats: 7g
Fiber: 5g | Cholesterol: 0mg | Sodium: 450mg | Potassium: 550mg

Crispy Baked Cauliflower Tacos

Prep. time: 15 min   Cook time: 25 min   Serves: 4

Ingredients
cauliflower one medium head, cut into florets
olive oil 2 tbsp
chili powder 1 tsp
paprika 1 tsp
cumin 1 tsp
garlic powder 1/2 tsp
sea salt 1/2 tsp
corn tortillas, eight small
Red cabbage 2 cups, shredded.
lime juice 2 tbsp, fresh
For the Sauce
vegan mayo 1/3 cup
lime juice 1 tbsp
hot sauce 1 tsp
Optional Toppings or Variations
sliced avocado for creaminess
chopped cilantro for freshness
pickled onions for tang

Directions
Prepare Cauliflower: Preheat the oven to 400°F (200°C). Toss cauliflower florets with olive oil, chili powder, paprika, cumin, garlic powder, and salt. Spread evenly on a baking sheet.
Bake Cauliflower: Roast cauliflower for 20-25 minutes, flipping halfway, until crispy and golden.
Make Sauce: Whisk vegan mayo, lime juice, and hot sauce until smooth in a small bowl.
Assemble Tacos: Warm corn tortillas. Fill each with roasted cauliflower, shredded red cabbage, and a drizzle of the sauce.
Serve: Garnish with optional toppings like avocado, cilantro, or pickled onions. Serve immediately.
Serving Suggestions
Pair with a side of black beans or quinoa salad for a hearty meal.

Nutritional Info (Per Serving)
Calories: 180 | Protein: 4g | Carbs: 19g | Fats: 8g
Fiber: 5g | Cholesterol: 0mg | Sodium: 450mg | Potassium: 600mg

Savory Stuffed Bell Peppers with Lentils

Prep. time: 15 min   Cook time: 30 min   Serves: 4

Ingredients

bell peppers four large, tops removed and seeds cleaned
cooked lentils 1 1/2 cups
cooked brown rice or quinoa 1 cup
olive oil 1 tbsp
Yellow onion, one medium, diced.
garlic two cloves, minced
tomato paste 2 tbsp
diced tomatoes one can (14 oz)
paprika 1 tsp
cumin 1 tsp
dried oregano 1/2 tsp
sea salt 1/2 tsp
black pepper 1/4 tsp
Optional Toppings or Variations
vegan cheese for topping
fresh parsley for garnish
crushed red pepper flakes for spice

Directions

Prepare Peppers: Preheat oven to 375°F (190°C). Place cleaned bell peppers upright in a baking dish.

Cook Filling: Heat olive oil in a skillet over medium heat. Sauté onion and garlic for 3-4 minutes until fragrant. Add tomato paste, diced tomatoes, lentils, rice or quinoa, paprika, cumin, oregano, salt, and pepper. Stir well and simmer for 5 minutes.

Stuff Peppers: Pack tightly the lentil mixture into each bell pepper. Cover the baking dish with foil.

Bake: Bake for 25-30 minutes until peppers are tender. If using vegan cheese, sprinkle on top during the last 5 minutes of baking.

Serve: Garnish with parsley or red pepper flakes if desired. Serve hot.

Serving Suggestions

Pair with a side salad or steamed vegetables for a balanced meal.

Nutritional Info (Per Serving)

Calories: 180 | Protein: 6g | Carbs: 28g | Fats: 4g
Fiber: 7g | Cholesterol: 0mg | Sodium: 450mg | Potassium: 750mg

Creamy Vegan Spinach and Artichoke Pasta

Prep. time: 10 min   Cook time: 20 min   Serves: 4

Ingredients

pasta 8 oz, any type
olive oil 1 tbsp
yellow onion, one small, diced
garlic three cloves, minced
unsweetened plant-based milk 1 1/2 cups
raw cashews 1/2 cup, soaked in water for 4 hours or boiled for 10 minutes
nutritional yeast 3 tbsp
lemon juice 1 tbsp, fresh
Artichoke hearts 1 cup, chopped.
fresh spinach 3 cups
sea salt 1/2 tsp
black pepper 1/4 tsp
Optional Toppings or Variations
red pepper flakes for heat
toasted pine nuts for crunch
chopped basil for freshness

Directions

Cook Pasta: Cook pasta according to package instructions. Rinse under cold water and drain.

Prepare Sauce: Blend soaked cashews, plant-based milk, nutritional yeast, lemon juice, salt, and pepper until smooth. Set it aside.

Cook Vegetables: Heat olive oil in a skillet over medium heat. Sauté onion and garlic for 3-4 minutes until soft and fragrant. Add artichoke hearts and cook for 2 minutes.

Combine Ingredients: Add spinach to the skillet and stir until wilted. Pour in the creamy sauce and stir to combine. Heat for 2-3 minutes.

Toss Pasta: Add cooked pasta to the skillet and toss until evenly coated with the sauce. Adjust seasoning if needed.

Serve: Garnish with optional toppings like red pepper flakes, pine nuts, or basil. Serve warmly.

Serving Suggestions

Pair with garlic bread or a simple green salad for a complete meal.

Nutritional Info (Per Serving)

Calories: 180 | Protein: 6g | Carbs: 28g | Fats: 4g
Fiber: 5g | Cholesterol: 0mg | Sodium: 450mg | Potassium: 600mg

Chapter 6: Comfort Foods Made Plant-Based

Classic Vegan Mac and Cheese

Prep. time: 10 min   Cook time: 20 min   Serves: 4

Ingredients

pasta 8 oz (macaroni or any preferred shape)
unsweetened plant-based milk 1 1/2 cups (e.g., almond, soy, or oat)
cashews 1/2 cup, soaked in water for 4 hours or boiled for 10 minutes
nutritional yeast 3 tbsp
lemon juice 1 tbsp, fresh
garlic powder 1 tsp
onion powder 1/2 tsp
turmeric 1/4 tsp (for color)
sea salt 1/2 tsp
black pepper 1/4 tsp
mustard powder 1 tsp (optional, for tang)
Optional Toppings or Variations
crispy breadcrumbs for topping
fresh parsley for garnish
smoked paprika for added flavor

Directions

Cook Noodles: Cook pasta according to package instructions. Rinse under cold water and drain.

To prepare the Sauce, Blend the soaked cashews, plant-based milk, nutritional yeast, lemon juice, garlic powder, onion powder, turmeric, salt, pepper, and mustard powder until smooth.

Heat Sauce: Pour the blended sauce into a saucepan and heat over medium heat, stirring constantly for 3-4 minutes until the sauce thickens.

Combine: Add the cooked pasta to the sauce and toss until fully coated.

Serve: Garnish with optional toppings such as crispy breadcrumbs, fresh parsley, or smoked paprika.

Serving Suggestions

Serve with a green salad or roasted vegetables for a satisfying meal.

Nutritional Info (Per Serving)

Calories: 180 | Protein: 6g | Carbs: 28g | Fats: 7g
Fiber: 3g | Cholesterol: 0mg | Sodium: 450mg | Potassium: 350mg

BBQ Jackfruit Pulled "Pork" Sandwiches

Prep. time: 15 min   Cook time: 25 min   Serves: 4

Ingredients

Young green jackfruit two cans (drained and shredded)
BBQ sauce 1 cup (preferably low-sugar or homemade)
olive oil 1 tbsp
yellow onion, one medium, finely chopped
garlic two cloves, minced
apple cider vinegar 1 tbsp
smoked paprika 1 tsp
ground cumin 1/2 tsp
salt 1/2 tsp
black pepper 1/4 tsp
sandwich buns 4 (whole-grain or gluten-free, if desired)
Optional Toppings or Variations
coleslaw (vegan)
pickles for crunch
avocado slices for added creaminess

Directions

Prepare Jackfruit: Drain and rinse jackfruit. Use your hands or two forks to shred it into pieces, removing any seeds or tricky bits.

Sauté Onions and Garlic: Heat olive oil in a skillet over medium heat. Add chopped onion and cook for 5 minutes until softened. Add minced garlic and cook for another minute.

Cook Jackfruit: Add shredded jackfruit to the skillet, stirring to combine with the onion and garlic. Cook for 3-4 minutes, allowing it to brown slightly.

Add BBQ Sauce: Stir in BBQ sauce, apple cider vinegar, smoked paprika, cumin, salt, and pepper. Simmer for 10-15 minutes, stirring occasionally, until the jackfruit is tender and well-coated with sauce.

Assemble Sandwiches: Toast sandwich buns if desired. Pile the BBQ jackfruit mixture onto the buns and top with optional coleslaw, pickles, or avocado slices.

Serve: Serve immediately with a side of roasted vegetables or a fresh salad for a complete meal.

Nutritional Info (Per Serving)

Calories: 300 | Protein: 6g | Carbs: 55g | Fats: 5g
Fiber: 6g | Cholesterol: 0mg | Sodium: 850mg | Potassium: 450mg

Dairy-Free Mashed Potatoes and Gravy

Prep. time: 10 min   Cook time: 20 min   Serves: 4

Ingredients

For the Mashed Potatoes:
russet potatoes four large, peeled and cubed
unsweetened plant-based milk 1/2 cup (e.g., almond, soy, or oat)
olive oil 2 tbsp
garlic powder 1/2 tsp
salt 1 tsp
black pepper 1/4 tsp
For the Gravy:
olive oil 2 tbsp
yellow onion one medium, chopped
garlic two cloves, minced
vegetable broth 2 cups
tamari or soy sauce 1 tbsp
nutritional yeast 2 tbsp
cornstarch 1 tbsp (mixed with 1 tbsp water)
thyme 1/2 tsp
black pepper 1/4 tsp

Directions

Cook Potatoes: Place cubed potatoes in a large pot and cover with water. Bring to a boil and cook for 12-15 minutes until tender when pierced with a fork. Drain well.
Mash Potatoes: In a large bowl, mash the potatoes with olive oil, plant-based milk, garlic powder, salt, and pepper until smooth and creamy. Adjust seasoning as needed.
Prepare the Gravy: Heat olive oil over medium heat in a skillet. Add chopped onion and cook for 5 minutes until softened. Add garlic and cook for another minute.
Make Gravy: Pour in vegetable broth, tamari, nutritional yeast, thyme, and black pepper. Stir well and bring to a simmer. In a small bowl, mix cornstarch with water and stir into the gravy. Cook for 3-5 minutes until the sauce thickens.
Serve: Spoon mashed potatoes onto plates and top with warm gravy. Garnish with fresh parsley or chopped chives if desired.

Nutritional Info (Per Serving)

Calories: 220 | Protein: 4g | Carbs: 35g | Fats: 8g
Fiber: 5g | Cholesterol: 0mg | Sodium: 650mg | Potassium: 600mg

Creamy Broccoli and "Cheddar" Soup

Prep. time: 10 min   Cook time: 20 min   Serves: 4

Ingredients

For the Soup:
broccoli florets 4 cups (about two small heads)
yellow onion one medium, chopped
carrots two medium, peeled and chopped
garlic three cloves, minced
unsweetened plant-based milk 2 cups (such as almond, soy, or oat)
vegetable broth 2 cups
Cashews 1/4 cup (soaked for 4-6 hours or use unsweetened cashew butter)
nutritional yeast 3 tbsp
turmeric 1/2 tsp
garlic powder 1/2 tsp
salt 1 tsp
black pepper 1/4 tsp
For Toppings (optional):
fresh parsley for garnish
croutons for added texture

Directions

Prepare Vegetables: Heat a little oil or water in a large pot over medium heat. Add the chopped onion and cook for 4-5 minutes until softened. Add garlic and cook for one more minute.
Cook Broccoli: Add the chopped carrots and broccoli to the pot. Pour vegetable broth and plant-based milk into the pot and bring the mixture to a simmer. Cook for 10-12 minutes until the vegetables are tender.
Blend Soup: Remove the pot from heat. Transfer the soup (in batches if necessary) to a high-speed blender. Add the soaked cashews (or cashew butter), nutritional yeast, turmeric, garlic powder, salt, and pepper. Blend until smooth and creamy.
Adjust Consistency: If the soup is too thick, add more plant-based milk or vegetable broth to reach your desired consistency. Taste and adjust seasoning if necessary.
Serve: Ladle the creamy soup into bowls. Top with fresh parsley and croutons if desired.

Nutritional Info (Per Serving)

Calories: 190 | Protein: 6g | Carbs: 22g | Fats: 10g
Fiber: 4g | Cholesterol: 0mg | Sodium: 650mg | Potassium: 600mg

Homemade Plant-Based Pizza with Cashew Mozzarella

Prep. time: 20 min   Cook time: 20 min   Serves: 4

Ingredients

For the Dough:
whole wheat flour 2 cups
warm water 3/4 cup
active dry yeast 1 tsp; olive oil 2 tbsp
Maple syrup 1 tsp; salt 1/2 tsp
For the Cashew Mozzarella:
Raw cashews 1 cup (soaked for 4 hours or use unsweetened cashew butter)
lemon juice 2 tbsp; garlic powder 1 tsp
nutritional yeast 3 tbsp
water 1/2 cup; salt 1/2 tsp
agar-agar powder 1 tsp
For the Toppings:
tomato sauce 1/2 cup (or more as desired)
fresh spinach 1 cup; olives 1/4 cup, sliced
Cherry tomatoes 1/2 cup, halved.
red onion 1/2 small, thinly sliced
Fresh basil leaves 1/4 cup, for garnish.

Directions

Prepare Dough: In a large bowl, combine warm water, maple syrup, and yeast. Let it sit for 5-10 minutes until frothy. Add flour, salt, and olive oil to the yeast mixture and stir until the dough forms. Knead for 5-7 minutes until smooth. Cover with a damp towel and let rise for 1 hour.
Make Cashew Mozzarella: Blend soaked cashews, lemon juice, nutritional yeast, garlic powder, water, salt, and agar-agar (if using) in a high-speed blender until smooth. If using agar-agar, heat the mixture in a saucepan over medium heat, stirring constantly until it thickens.
Shape and Preheat: Preheat the oven to 475°F (245°C). Divide the dough into two equal portions and roll each into a pizza shape on a floured surface. Place on a parchment-lined baking sheet or pizza stone.
Assemble Pizza: Spread a thin layer of tomato sauce on each pizza crust. Add the cashew mozzarella, fresh spinach, cherry tomatoes, red onion, and olives.
Bake: Place the pizzas in the oven and bake for 15-20 minutes, until the crust is golden and the cheese is bubbly.

Nutritional Info (Per Serving)

Calories: 320 | Protein: 8g | Carbs: 45g | Fats: 14g
Fiber: 6g | Cholesterol: 0mg | Sodium: 700mg | Potassium: 550mg

Vegan Pot Pie with Flaky Crust

Prep. time: 10 min   Cook time: 10 min   Serves: 2

Ingredients

For the Filling:
olive oil 2 tbsp
yellow onion, one medium diced
carrots two medium, diced; celery, two stalks, diced
garlic three cloves, minced
frozen peas 1 cup
potatoes two medium, peeled and cubed
vegetable broth 2 cups
canned coconut milk 1/2 cup
all-purpose flour 3 tbsp
dried thyme 1 tsp; dried rosemary 1 tsp
black pepper 1/2 tsp;
salt 1 tsp
For the Flaky Crust:
all-purpose flour 1 1/2 cups
vegan butter 1/2 cup, chilled and cubed
cold water 4-6 tbsp
salt 1/4 tsp

Directions

Prepare Filling: Heat olive oil in a large pan over medium heat. Add diced onion, carrots, and celery, cooking until softened, about 5-7 minutes. Add garlic and cook for one more minute. Sprinkle flour over the vegetables and stir well to combine. Gradually add vegetable broth, coconut milk, thyme, rosemary, salt, and pepper, stirring continuously. Bring to a simmer and cook for 5-7 minutes until the sauce thickens. Add frozen peas and cubed potatoes. Simmer for 10-15 minutes until the potatoes are tender.
Make the Crust: In a large bowl, combine flour and salt. Cut in chilled vegan butter using a pastry cutter or fork until the mixture resembles coarse crumbs. Gradually add cold water, 1 tbsp, mixing until a dough forms. Wrap the dough in plastic and refrigerate for 30 minutes.
Assemble the Pot Pie: Preheat the oven to 400°F (200°C). Roll out the dough on a floured surface to fit the top of a 9-inch pie dish. Pour the vegetable filling into the dish. Place the rolled dough on top, trimming any excess and crimping the edges. Cut a few slits in the top to allow steam to escape.
Bake: Place the pot pie in the oven and bake for 30-35 minutes

Nutritional Info (Per Serving): Calories: 290 | Protein: 6g | Carbs: 38g | Fats: 14g |
Fiber: 6g | Cholesterol: 0mg | Sodium: 700mg | Potassium: 800mg

Crispy Fried "Chicken" Tofu Strips

Prep. time: 20 min   Cook time: 15 min   Serves: 4

Ingredients

For the Tofu Strips:
firm tofu 14 oz, drained and pressed
all-purpose flour 1/2 cup
cornstarch 1/4 cup
garlic powder 1 tsp
onion powder 1 tsp
smoked paprika 1 tsp
salt 1/2 tsp
black pepper 1/4 tsp
plant-based milk 1/2 cup
hot sauce 1 tbsp (optional)
For Frying:
vegetable oil 1-2 cups, for frying

Directions

Prepare the Tofu: Slice the pressed tofu into strips (about 1/2 inch wide).
Coat the Tofu: In a shallow bowl, mix flour, cornstarch, garlic powder, onion powder, smoked paprika, salt, and black pepper. In another bowl, whisk together the plant-based milk and hot sauce (if using). Dip each tofu strip into the wet mixture and then coat thoroughly in the dry flour mixture.
Fry the Tofu: Heat vegetable oil in a large skillet over medium-high heat. Once hot, carefully place the coated tofu strips into the oil. Fry in batches, cooking each strip for 3-4 minutes until golden and crispy. Remove the tofu strips from the skillet and place them on a paper towel-lined plate to drain excess oil.
Serve: You can serve the crispy tofu strips as is or with your favorite dipping sauce, such as vegan ranch or BBQ sauce.

Nutritional Info (Per Serving)
Calories: 220 | Protein: 12g | Carbs: 18g | Fats: 14g
Fiber: 2g | Cholesterol: 0mg | Sodium: 600mg | Potassium: 250mg

Smoky Vegan Sloppy Joes

Prep. time: 10 min   Cook time: 20 min   Serves: 4

Ingredients

For the Sloppy Joes:
cooked lentils 1 1/2 cups
Onion one medium diced
green bell pepper 1, diced
garlic three cloves, minced
tomato paste 2 tbsp
tomato sauce 1 cup
BBQ sauce 1/4 cup
liquid smoke 1 tsp
smoked paprika 1 tsp
soy sauce or tamari 1 tbsp
cayenne pepper 1/4 tsp (optional)
salt 1/2 tsp
black pepper 1/4 tsp
olive oil 1 tbsp
For Serving:
whole wheat burger buns 4

Directions

Prepare the Veggies: Heat olive oil in a skillet over medium heat. Add the diced onion, bell pepper, and garlic. Sauté for 5-7 minutes, until softened.
Make the Sloppy Joe Mixture: Add the tomato paste, tomato sauce, BBQ sauce, liquid smoke, smoked paprika, soy sauce, cayenne pepper, salt, and black pepper. Stir well to combine. Add the cooked lentils and simmer for 10-15 minutes, allowing the flavors to meld and the mixture to thicken.
If desired, spoon the smoky lentil mixture onto the bottom half of each bun to assemble the Sloppy Joes and toast the burger buns.
Serve Top with additional toppings, such as sliced pickles or coleslaw, for extra flavor and crunch. Serve with a side of veggies or baked fries.

Nutritional Info (Per Serving)
Calories: 290 | Protein: 16g | Carbs: 45g | Fats: 7g
Fiber: 12g | Cholesterol: 0mg | Sodium: 850mg | Potassium: 550mg

Savory Vegan Lasagna with Cashew Ricotta

Prep. time: 20 min   Cook time: 45 min   Serves: 6

Ingredients

For the Cashew Ricotta:
raw cashews (soaked for at least 2 hours or overnight) 1 cup
lemon juice 2 tbsp
nutritional yeast 2 tbsp
garlic powder 1 tsp
salt 1/2 tsp
water 1/4 cup
For the Lasagna Layers:
lasagna noodles (gluten-free if preferred) 9 sheets
marinara sauce 3 cups
fresh spinach 2 cups, chopped
zucchini 1, sliced thin
mushrooms 1 cup, sliced
onion one medium diced
garlic two cloves, minced
olive oil 1 tbsp
dried basil 1 tsp
dried oregano 1 tsp
salt and pepper to taste

Directions

Prepare the Cashew Ricotta: Blend the soaked cashews, lemon juice, nutritional yeast, garlic powder, salt, and water in a high-speed blender until smooth and creamy. Set aside.

Prepare the Vegetables: Heat olive oil over medium heat in a skillet. Add the onion, garlic, zucchini, and mushrooms. Sauté for 5-7 minutes until softened. Add spinach and cook for an additional 2 minutes until wilted. Stir in dried basil, oregano, salt, and pepper.

Cook Noodles: Cook the lasagna noodles according to package instructions. Drain and set aside.

Assemble the Lasagna: Preheat the oven to 375°F (190°C). Spread a thin layer of marinara sauce on the bottom of a 9x13-inch baking dish. Layer 3 lasagna noodles, followed by half of the sautéed vegetable mixture, half of the cashew ricotta, and more marinara sauce. Repeat with the remaining noodles, vegetables, cashew ricotta, and sauce.

Bake: Cover the lasagna with aluminum foil and bake for 30 minutes. Remove the foil and bake for 15 minutes until the top is slightly golden. Let it cool for 5-10 minutes before serving.

Serve: Slice the lasagna and serve with a side salad or steamed vegetables.

Nutritional Info (Per Serving)

Calories: 350 | Protein: 14g | Carbs: 42g | Fats: 15g
Fiber: 6g | Cholesterol: 0mg | Sodium: 550mg | Potassium: 650mg

Cheesy Baked Cauliflower Casserole

Prep. time: 15 min   Cook time: 35 min   Serves: 6

Ingredients

For the Casserole:
cauliflower florets 4 cups
olive oil 1 tbsp; sea salt 1/2 tsp
garlic powder 1 tsp
onion powder 1 tsp
nutritional yeast 3 tbsp
fresh ground black pepper 1/4 tsp
For the Vegan Cheese Sauce:
cashews (soaked for at least 2 hours) 1 cup
unsweetened almond milk 1 cup
nutritional yeast 1/4 cup
lemon juice 2 tbsp
garlic two cloves
turmeric 1/2 tsp; sea salt 1/2 tsp
ground mustard 1/2 tsp

Directions

Prepare the Cauliflower: Preheat the oven to 375°F (190°C). Toss the cauliflower florets with olive oil, garlic powder, onion powder, nutritional yeast, salt, and black pepper. Spread the cauliflower evenly on a baking sheet and roast for 20-25 minutes, flipping halfway through.

Make the Cheese Sauce: While the cauliflower is roasting, blend the soaked cashews, almond milk, nutritional yeast, lemon juice, garlic, turmeric, salt, and ground mustard in a high-speed blender until smooth and creamy.

Assemble the Casserole: Once the cauliflower is done roasting, transfer it to a baking dish. Pour the vegan cheese sauce over the cauliflower, tossing gently to coat. If using, sprinkle the vegan breadcrumbs over the top for a crispy finish.

Bake: Return the casserole to the oven for 10 minutes until bubbly and golden.

Nutritional Info (Per Serving)

Calories: 220 | Protein: 6g | Carbs: 18g | Fats: 15g
Fiber: 6g | Cholesterol: 0mg | Sodium: 500mg | Potassium: 600mg

Hearty Vegan Chili with Cornbread Topping

Prep. time: 15 min   Cook time: 45 min   Serves: 6

Ingredients

For the Chili:

olive oil 2 tbsp; garlic cloves (minced) 3

yellow onion (diced) 1 medium

red bell pepper (diced) 1

carrots (diced) 2; tomato paste 2 tbsp

canned diced tomatoes (with juice) 2 cans (14 oz)

vegetable broth 2 cups

black beans (drained and rinsed) 1 can (15 oz)

kidney beans (drained and rinsed) 1 can (15 oz)

corn kernels (frozen or canned) 1 cup

chili powder 2 tbsp; cumin 1 tsp

smoked paprika 1 tsp; salt 1 tsp

cocoa powder 1 tsp; pepper 1/2 tsp

For the Cornbread Topping:

cornmeal 1 cup; baking powder 1 tsp

all-purpose flour 1/2 cup; salt 1/4 tsp

unsweetened almond milk 1 cup

apple cider vinegar 1 tsp

maple syrup 2 tbsp; olive oil 2 tbsp

Directions

Heat olive oil in a large pot over medium heat to prepare Chili. Sauté onion, garlic, bell pepper, and carrots for 5-7 minutes until softened.

Add Spices and Tomato Paste: Stir in chili powder, cumin, smoked paprika, and cocoa powder. Cook for 1 minute to toast the spices. Add tomato paste and mix well.

Simmer: Add diced tomatoes, vegetable broth, black beans, kidney beans, and corn—season with salt and pepper. Bring to a boil, then reduce heat to low and simmer for 30 minutes, stirring occasionally.

Prepare Cornbread Batter: In a bowl, whisk cornmeal, flour, baking powder, and salt. Mix almond milk, apple cider vinegar, maple syrup, and olive oil in another bowl. Combine wet and dry ingredients, stirring until smooth.

Assemble and Bake: Preheat the oven to 400°F (200°C). Pour the chili into a large oven-safe dish. Spread the cornbread batter evenly over the top. Bake for 20-25 minutes or until the cornbread is golden brown and cooked.

Serve: Let cool slightly before serving. Garnish with fresh cilantro, avocado slices, or a dollop of vegan sour cream if desired.

Nutritional Info (Per Serving)

Calories: 320 | Protein: 10g | Carbs: 50g | Fats: 9g

Fiber: 11g | Cholesterol: 0mg | Sodium: 680mg | Potassium: 700mg

Golden Shepherd's Pie with Creamy Potato Crust

Prep. time: 20 min   Cook time: 40 min   Serves: 6

Ingredients

For the Potato Crust:

russet potatoes (peeled and cubed) 4 large

unsweetened almond milk 1/2 cup

vegan butter 2 tbsp

salt 1/2 tsp; pepper 1/4 tsp

For the Filling:

olive oil 2 tbsp; carrots (diced) 2

yellow onion (diced) 1 medium

celery stalks (diced) 2

garlic cloves (minced) 3

mushrooms (finely chopped) 2 cups

lentils (cooked or canned) 2 cups

frozen peas 1 cup; tomato paste 2 tbsp

vegetable broth 1 cup

soy sauce 1 tbsp; thyme 1 tsp

smoked paprika 1/2 tsp

cornstarch (mixed with 2 tbsp water) 1 tbsp

salt 1/2 tsp; pepper 1/4 tsp

Directions

Cook Potatoes: Boil potatoes in salted water until tender, about 15 minutes. Drain and mash with almond milk, vegan butter, salt, and pepper until creamy. Set aside.

Prepare Filling: Heat olive oil in a large skillet over medium heat. Sauté onion, carrots, and celery for 5-7 minutes until softened. Add garlic and mushrooms, cooking for five more minutes.

Add Lentils and Seasonings: Stir in lentils, tomato paste, soy sauce, thyme, smoked paprika, salt, and pepper. Mix well.

Simmer: Add vegetable broth and peas. Simmer for 10 minutes. Stir in the cornstarch mixture to thicken the filling. Adjust seasoning if needed.

Assemble: Preheat oven to 400°F (200°C). Spread the filling evenly in a baking dish. Layer the mashed potatoes on top, smoothing with a spatula.

Bake: Bake for 20-25 minutes or until the top is lightly golden. If desired, broil for 2-3 minutes for a crispier crust.

Serve: Let cool slightly before serving. Garnish with fresh parsley or chives for added flavor.

Nutritional Info (Per Serving)

Calories: 290 | Protein: 9g | Carbs: 48g | Fats: 7g

Fiber: 9g | Cholesterol: 0mg | Sodium: 580mg | Potassium: 850mg

Classic Stuffed Shells with Spinach and Cashew Cream

Prep. time: 15 min   Cook time: 45 min   Serves: 4

Ingredients

For the Stuffed Shells:
12 large pasta shells
2 cups spinach (fresh or frozen)
1/2 cup raw cashews (soaked for 4 hours or overnight)
1/2 cup water
1/2 cup nutritional yeast
1 tbsp lemon juice
One garlic clove
1/2 tsp salt, 1/4 tsp pepper
For the Marinara Sauce:
2 cups marinara sauce (store-bought or homemade)
1 tsp dried oregano
1/2 tsp red pepper flakes (optional)

Directions

Cook Pasta: Boil pasta shells according to package instructions. Drain and set aside.
To make cashew cream, blend soaked cashews, water, nutritional yeast, lemon juice, garlic, salt, and pepper in a blender until smooth.
Prepare Filling: Sauté spinach until wilted, then mix with cashew cream to form the filling.
Assemble Shells: Stuff each shell with the spinach-cashew cream mixture and place in a baking dish.
Add Sauce: Pour the marinara sauce on overstuffed shells and sprinkle with oregano and red pepper flakes (if using).
Bake: Cover with foil and bake at 375°F for 25-30 minutes. Remove foil and bake for an additional 5 minutes.

Nutritional Info (Per Serving)
Calories: 300 | Protein: 10g | Carbs: 39g | Fats: 12g
Fiber: 6g | Cholesterol: 0mg | Sodium: 550mg | Potassium: 650mg

Warm and Cheesy Vegan Garlic Breadsticks

Prep. time: 15 min   Cook time: 20 min   Serves: 8 breadsticks

Ingredients

For the Breadsticks:
1 cup warm water (110°F)
1 tbsp active dry yeast
1 tbsp maple syrup
2 1/2 cups all-purpose flour
1/2 tsp salt; 1 tbsp olive oil
For the Garlic Topping:
3 tbsp vegan butter, melted
Two garlic cloves, minced
1/4 tsp dried oregano; 1/4 tsp salt
1/4 tsp dried basil
For the Vegan Cheese:
1/2 cup unsweetened plant-based milk
1/4 cup nutritional yeast
1 tbsp all-purpose flour
1/4 tsp garlic powder
1/4 tsp onion powder
Pinch of salt and pepper

Directions

Prepare Dough: In a bowl, combine warm water, yeast, and maple syrup. Let sit for 5 minutes until it is bubbly. Add flour, salt, and olive oil, mixing to form dough. Knead for 5-7 minutes until smooth. Cover and let rise for 1 hour.
Shape the Dough: Preheat the oven to 375°F (190°C). Roll out the dough on a floured surface into a rectangle. Cut it into eight strips.
Make Vegan Cheese: In a small pot, whisk together plant-based milk, nutritional yeast, flour, garlic powder, onion powder, salt, and pepper. Cook over medium heat, stirring until thickened (about 3-5 minutes).
Assemble Breadsticks: Place dough strips on a greased baking sheet. Brush with melted vegan butter, then sprinkle with garlic, salt, oregano, and basil. Spoon vegan cheese over the breadsticks.
Bake: Bake for 12-15 minutes or until golden brown.

Nutritional Info (Per Serving)
Calories: 180 | Protein: 4g | Carbs: 30g | Fats: 7g
Fiber: 2g | Cholesterol: 0mg | Sodium: 450mg | Potassium: 150mg

Chapter 7: Desserts and Sweet Treats

Chocolate-Dipped Coconut Macaroons

Prep. time: 15 min   Setting time: 30 min   Serves: 12 macaroons

Ingredients

For the Macaroons:
2 1/2 cups unsweetened shredded coconut
1/4 cup maple syrup
1/4 cup coconut flour
1 tsp vanilla extract
1/4 tsp sea salt
2 tbsp aquafaba (chickpea brine) or flaxseed meal
For the Chocolate Dip:
1/2 cup dairy-free dark chocolate chips
1 tbsp coconut oil

Directions

Preheat Oven: Preheat the oven to 350°F (175°C). Line a baking sheet with parchment paper.
Prepare Macaroon Mixture: In a large bowl, combine shredded coconut, maple syrup, coconut flour, vanilla extract, sea salt, and aquafaba (or flaxseed meal). Stir until well combined and sticky.
Shape Macaroons: Using your hands, form the mixture into small mounds, about 1 1/2 inches tall, and place them on the prepared baking sheet.
Bake: Bake the macaroons for 15-18 minutes or until golden brown on the edges. Let them cool on the baking sheet for 10 minutes before transferring to a wire rack.
Prepare Chocolate Dip: While the macaroons cool, melt the dark chocolate chips and coconut oil in a heatproof bowl over a double boiler or microwave in 30-second intervals, stirring in between until smooth.
Dip Macaroons: Once the macaroons are cooled, dip the bottoms of each macaroon into the melted chocolate, then return them to the wire rack to allow the chocolate to set.
Set and Serve: Let the chocolate-dipped macaroons set for 20 minutes or refrigerate for a faster setting. Serve at room temperature or chilled.

Nutritional Info (Per Serving)
Calories: 180 | Protein: 2g | Carbs: 22g | Fats: 11g
Fiber: 3g | Cholesterol: 0mg | Sodium: 30mg | Potassium: 125mg

Maple Cinnamon Roasted Pears with Walnuts

Prep. time: 10 min   Setting time: 25 min   Serves: 4

Ingredients

Four ripe pears, halved and cored
2 tbsp maple syrup
1 tsp ground cinnamon
1/2 tsp ground ginger
1/4 tsp vanilla extract
1 tbsp coconut oil, melted
1/4 cup chopped walnuts
A pinch of sea salt

Directions

Preheat Oven: Preheat the oven to 375°F (190°C). Line a baking sheet with parchment paper.
Prepare Pears: Slice the pears in half, remove the cores, and cut them side up on the prepared baking sheet.
Make Maple Cinnamon Mixture: In a small bowl, combine maple syrup, cinnamon, ginger, vanilla extract, and melted coconut oil. Stir well.
Roast Pears: Brush the pear halves with the maple cinnamon mixture. Sprinkle chopped walnuts over the pears.
Bake: Roast the pears in the oven for 20-25 minutes or until tender and slightly caramelized.
Serve: Remove the pears from the oven, sprinkle with a pinch of sea salt, and serve warm. Optionally, drizzle with extra maple syrup for added sweetness.

Nutritional Info (Per Serving)
Calories: 180 | Protein: 2g | Carbs: 35g | Fats: 8g
Fiber: 5g | Cholesterol: 0mg | Sodium: 10mg | Potassium: 270mg

Vegan S'mores Bars with Almond Butter

Prep. time: 15 min   Setting time: 2 hour   Serves: 12

Ingredients

1 1/2 cups rolled oats
1 cup almond flour
1/4 cup maple syrup
1/2 cup almond butter
1 tsp vanilla extract
1/4 tsp sea salt
1/2 cup dairy-free chocolate chips
1/4 cup mini marshmallows (vegan)

Directions

Prepare the Base: In a large mixing bowl, combine the rolled oats, almond flour, maple syrup, almond butter, vanilla extract, and sea salt. Stir until the mixture is well combined and sticky.

Press into Pan: Line an 8x8-inch baking pan with parchment paper. Press the oat mixture into the bottom of the pan to form an even base.

Add Chocolate and Marshmallows: Sprinkle the chocolate chips evenly over the oat base. Then, top with mini vegan marshmallows.

Chill: Place the pan in the refrigerator for at least 2 hours to allow the bars to set.

Serve: Once set, slice into squares and serve. These bars are perfect as a snack or dessert!

Nutritional Info (Per Serving)

Calories: 180 | Protein: 4g | Carbs: 20g | Fats: 9g
Fiber: 4g | Cholesterol: 0mg | Sodium: 50mg | Potassium: 150mg

Sweet Potato and Chocolate Chip Blondies

Prep. time: 15 min   Bake time: 30 min   Serves: 12

Ingredients

One medium sweet potato, peeled and cubed
1 cup almond flour
1/2 cup maple syrup
1/4 cup coconut oil, melted
1 tsp vanilla extract
1/2 tsp baking soda
1/4 tsp sea salt
1/2 cup dairy-free chocolate chips
1/4 cup chopped walnuts (optional)

Directions

Cook Sweet Potato: Steam or boil the sweet potato cubes for 10-12 minutes until tender. Drain and mash until smooth.

Prepare Blondie Batter: In a large bowl, mix the mashed sweet potato, almond flour, maple syrup, melted coconut oil, vanilla extract, baking soda, and sea salt. Stir until well combined.

Add Chocolate Chips: Fold in the chocolate chips and chopped walnuts.

Bake: Preheat oven to 350°F (175°C). Grease or line an 8x8-inch baking pan with parchment paper. Pour the batter into the pan and spread evenly. Bake for 30 minutes or until a toothpick comes out clean.

Cool and Serve: Allow to cool completely before cutting into squares. Serve and enjoy!

Nutritional Info (Per Serving)

Calories: 180 | Protein: 3g | Carbs: 25g | Fats: 9g
Fiber: 4g | Cholesterol: 0mg | Sodium: 150mg | Potassium: 300mg

Decadent Vegan Chocolate Brownies

Prep. time: 15 min   Cook time: 25-30 min   Serves: 12

Ingredients

For the Brownies:
whole wheat flour 1 cup
cocoa powder (unsweetened) 1/3 cup
baking powder 1 tsp
sea salt 1/4 tsp
Maple syrup 1/2 cup
unsweetened applesauce 1/4 cup
almond milk 1/4 cup
vanilla extract 1 tsp
ground flaxseed 1 tbsp (mixed with 3 tbsp water
to form a flax egg)
dark chocolate chips (dairy-free) 1/2 cup
Optional Toppings:
chopped walnuts 1/4 cup
shredded coconut 2 tbsp

Directions

Prepare the Flax Egg: In a small bowl, mix the ground flaxseed with 3 tbsp of water. Stir well and let it sit for 5 minutes to form a gel-like consistency.
Mix the Dry Ingredients: In a medium bowl, whisk together the whole wheat flour, cocoa powder, baking powder, and sea salt.
Mix the Wet Ingredients: In a large bowl, combine the maple syrup, applesauce, almond milk, vanilla extract, and flax egg. Stir well.
Combine Wet and Dry Ingredients: Gradually add the dry ingredients to the wet ingredients, stirring until thoroughly combined. Fold in the chocolate chips.
Prepare the Pan: Preheat the oven to 350°F (175°C). Line an 8x8-inch baking pan with parchment paper or lightly grease it. Pour the brownie batter into the pan, spreading it out evenly.
Bake: Bake for 25-30 minutes or until a toothpick inserted into the center comes out clean. Let the brownies cool in the pan for 10 minutes before transferring to a wire rack.
Serve: Cut into 12 squares and serve. Optionally, top with chopped walnuts or shredded coconut for added texture and flavor.

Nutritional Info (Per Serving)
Calories: 180 | Protein: 3g | Carbs: 28g | Fats: 8g
Fiber: 4g | Cholesterol: 0mg | Sodium: 200mg | Potassium: 180mg

Fresh Berry Vegan Cheesecake Bars

Prep. time: 20 min   Setting time: 4 hours   Serves: 12

Ingredients

For the Crust:
rolled oats 1 cup; sea salt 1/4 tsp
almonds (or walnuts) 1/2 cup
maple syrup 2 tbsp
coconut oil (melted) 2 tbsp
For the Filling:
Raw cashews 1 1/2 cups (soaked in hot water for
1 hour, then drained)
coconut cream 1/2 cup
lemon juice 1/4 cup
maple syrup 1/3 cup; vanilla extract 1 tsp
For the Berry Topping:
mixed fresh berries (blueberries, raspberries, sliced
strawberries) 1 1/2 cups
chia seeds 1 tbsp
Maple syrup 1 tbsp

Directions

Prepare the Crust: Blend the oats and almonds until finely ground in a food processor. Add maple syrup, melted coconut oil, and sea salt. Blend until the mixture holds together when pressed. Press the mixture evenly into an 8x8-inch pan lined with parchment paper.
Prepare the Filling: Blend the soaked and drained cashews, coconut cream, lemon juice, maple syrup, and vanilla extract in a high-speed blender until smooth and creamy. Pour the filling over the crust and spread evenly.
Prepare the Berry Topping: In a small bowl, mash the fresh berries with a fork until juicy but slightly chunky. Stir in chia seeds and maple syrup. Let the mixture sit for 5 minutes, then spread evenly over the cheesecake filling.
Set: Cover the pan and refrigerate for at least 4 hours or until the bars are firm.
Serve: Slice into 12 bars. Serve chilled, optionally topped with extra fresh berries or a drizzle of maple syrup.

Nutritional Info (Per Serving)
Calories: 180 | Protein: 4g | Carbs: 17g | Fats: 12g
Fiber: 3g | Cholesterol: 0mg | Sodium: 50mg | Potassium: 190mg

Creamy Coconut Rice Pudding

Prep. time: 5 min   Cook time: 25 min   Serves: 4

Ingredients

cooked jasmine rice 1 cup
full-fat coconut milk one can (13.5 oz)
maple syrup 2 tbsp
vanilla extract 1 tsp
ground cinnamon 1/2 tsp
sea salt 1/4 tsp

Optional Toppings:

sliced almonds 2 tbsp
fresh mango or berries 1/2 cup
shredded coconut 1 tbsp

Directions

Combine Ingredients: In a medium saucepan, combine the cooked rice, coconut milk, maple syrup, vanilla extract, cinnamon, and sea salt. Stir well.

Cook Pudding: Bring the mixture to a gentle simmer over medium heat, stirring occasionally. Reduce heat to low and cook for about 20 minutes, stirring frequently, until the mixture thickens to a creamy consistency.

Cool Slightly: Remove from heat and let the pudding cool for 5 minutes. It will continue to thicken as it cools.

Serve: Divide the pudding into four bowls. Top with sliced almonds, fresh fruit, or shredded coconut as desired. Serve warm or chilled.

Nutritional Info (Per Serving)

Calories: 180 | Protein: 3g | Carbs: 16g | Fats: 13g
Fiber: 4g | Cholesterol: 0mg | Sodium: 100mg | Potassium: 180mg

Flourless Peanut Butter Cookies

Prep. time: 5 min   Cook time: 10 min   Serves: 12

Ingredients

natural creamy peanut butter 1 cup
coconut sugar 3/4 cup
flaxseed meal 1 tbsp (mixed with 2.5 tbsp water)
vanilla extract 1 tsp
baking soda 1/2 tsp
sea salt 1/4 tsp

Optional Toppings:

dark chocolate chips 1/4 cup
crushed peanuts 2 tbsp

Directions

Preheat Oven: Preheat your oven to 350°F (175°C) and line a baking sheet with parchment paper.

Prepare Flax Egg: Combine flaxseed meal with water in a small bowl. Let it sit for 5 minutes until it forms a gel-like consistency.

Mix Dough: In a mixing bowl, combine peanut butter, coconut sugar, flax egg, vanilla extract, baking soda, and sea salt. Stir until a smooth dough forms.

Shape Cookies: Scoop one tablespoon of dough for each cookie, roll into balls, and place on the prepared baking sheet. Press down slightly with a fork to create a crisscross pattern.

Bake: Bake in the preheated oven for 9–10 minutes. Allow the cookies to cool on the baking sheet for 5 minutes before transferring them to a wire rack.

Serve: Enjoy as-is or top with a sprinkle of crushed peanuts or melted dark chocolate drizzle.

Nutritional Info (Per Serving)

Calories: 180 | Protein: 4g | Carbs: 12g | Fats: 14g
Fiber: 3g | Cholesterol: 0mg | Sodium: 140mg | Potassium: 200mg

Classic Plant-Based Banana Bread

Prep. time: 10 min   Cook time: 50-60 min   Serves: 8

Ingredients

ripe bananas, three large, mashed
all-purpose flour 1 1/2 cups
coconut sugar 1/2 cup
unsweetened almond milk 1/4 cup
neutral oil (e.g., avocado oil) 1/4 cup
vanilla extract 1 tsp
baking soda 1 tsp
baking powder 1/2 tsp
cinnamon 1 tsp
sea salt 1/4 tsp
Optional Add-Ins:
chopped walnuts 1/4 cup
dark chocolate chips 1/4 cup

Directions

Preheat Oven: Preheat the oven to 350°F (175°C) and grease or line a loaf pan with parchment paper.

Mash Bananas: Mash the ripe bananas until smooth in a large mixing bowl.

Mix Wet Ingredients: Add coconut sugar, almond milk, oil, and vanilla extract to the mashed bananas. Stir until well combined.

Combine Dry Ingredients: In a separate bowl, whisk together flour, baking soda, baking powder, cinnamon, and salt.

Mix Batter: Gradually fold the dry ingredients into the wet mixture. Stir until just combined. If desired, add optional walnuts or chocolate chips.

Bake: Pour the batter into the prepared loaf pan. Smooth the top and bake for 50–60 minutes, or until a toothpick inserted in the center comes out clean.

Cool: Let the banana bread cool in the pan for 10 minutes before transferring it to a wire rack to cool completely.

Serve: Slice and enjoy as a wholesome snack or breakfast. Pair with plant-based butter or nut butter for extra flavor.

Nutritional Info (Per Serving)

Calories: 180 | Protein: 3g | Carbs: 30g | Fats: 6g
Fiber: 3g | Cholesterol: 0mg | Sodium: 180mg | Potassium: 300mg

Chocolate Avocado Mousse

Prep. time: 10 min   Chill time: 30 min   Serves: 4

Ingredients

ripe avocados, two medium, peeled and pitted
unsweetened cocoa powder 1/4 cup
Maple syrup 1/4 cup
unsweetened almond milk 1/4 cup
vanilla extract 1 tsp
pinch of sea salt
Optional Toppings:
fresh berries
shredded coconut
chopped nuts

Directions

Blend Ingredients: Place the avocados, cocoa powder, maple syrup, almond milk, vanilla extract, and salt in a blender or food processor. Blend until smooth and creamy, scraping down the sides as needed.

Adjust Sweetness: Taste the mousse and adjust sweetness with more maple syrup if desired.

Chill: Transfer the mousse into individual serving bowls or ramekins. Cover and refrigerate for at least 30 minutes to allow the flavors to meld.

Serve: Garnish with optional toppings like fresh berries, shredded coconut, or chopped nuts. Serve chilled.

Nutritional Info (Per Serving)

Calories: 180 | Protein: 3g | Carbs: 16g | Fats: 13g
Fiber: 5g | Cholesterol: 0mg | Sodium: 50mg | Potassium: 400mg

No-Bake Vegan Lemon Tarts

Prep. time: 20 min   Chill time: 1 hour   Serves: 6

Ingredients
Crust
almonds 1 cup
Dates 1/2 cup, pitted
shredded unsweetened coconut 1/4 cup
Filling
raw cashews 1 cup, soaked in hot water for 30 minutes and drained
coconut cream 1/2 cup
Maple syrup 1/4 cup
lemon juice 1/4 cup (about two lemons)
lemon zest 1 tsp
turmeric powder 1/4 tsp (for color)
Optional Toppings
fresh raspberries
mint leaves
extra lemon zest

Directions
Prepare the Crust: In a food processor, blend almonds, dates, and shredded coconut until the mixture sticks together when pressed. Divide the mixture evenly into tart molds or a muffin tin lined with parchment paper. Press firmly to form crusts.
Blend the Filling: In a blender, combine soaked cashews, coconut cream, maple syrup, lemon juice, lemon zest, and turmeric powder. Blend until smooth and creamy.
Assemble the Tarts: Spoon the filling over the prepared crusts, smoothing the tops with a spoon.
Chill: Refrigerate the tarts for at least 1 hour to set.
Serve: Garnish with optional toppings like fresh raspberries, mint leaves, or additional lemon zest. Serve chilled.

Nutritional Info (Per Serving)
Calories: 180 | Protein: 3g | Carbs: 16g | Fats: 13g
Fiber: 4g | Cholesterol: 0mg | Sodium: 15mg | Potassium: 320mg

Apple Cinnamon Crumble with Oat Topping

Prep. time: 15 min   Cook time: 30 min   Serves: 6

Ingredients
Filling
apples four medium, peeled, cored, and sliced
Maple syrup 3 tbsp
lemon juice 1 tbsp
cinnamon 1 tsp
nutmeg 1/4 tsp
Topping
rolled oats 1 cup
almond flour 1/2 cup
Coconut oil 1/4 cup, melted.
maple syrup 2 tbsp
cinnamon 1/2 tsp
Optional Toppings
chopped pecans
vegan vanilla ice cream

Directions
Prepare the Filling: Preheat the oven to 350°F (175°C). Toss apple slices with maple syrup, lemon juice, cinnamon, and nutmeg in a mixing bowl. Transfer to a greased baking dish.
Make the Topping: In another bowl, combine rolled oats, almond flour, melted coconut oil, maple syrup, and cinnamon. Mix until crumbly.
Assemble the Crumble: Spread the oat topping evenly over the apple mixture, pressing slightly to adhere.
Bake: Place the dish in the oven for 30 minutes or until the apples are tender and the topping is golden brown.
Serve: Let cool slightly before serving. Garnish with chopped pecans or a scoop of vegan vanilla ice cream for added flavor.

Nutritional Info (Per Serving)
Calories: 180 | Protein: 3g | Carbs: 16g | Fats: 13g
Fiber: 4g | Cholesterol: 0mg | Sodium: 10mg | Potassium: 350mg

Pumpkin Spice Vegan Cupcakes

Prep. time: 15 min   Cook time: 25 min   Serves: 12

Ingredients

Cupcakes
all-purpose flour 1 1/2 cups
pumpkin puree 1 cup
Maple syrup 1/2 cup
unsweetened almond milk 1/2 cup
Coconut oil 1/4 cup, melted.
baking powder 1 tsp
baking soda 1/2 tsp
pumpkin pie spice 1 1/2 tsp
vanilla extract 1 tsp
salt 1/4 tsp
Frosting (optional)
coconut cream 1 cup, chilled and whipped
maple syrup 2 tbsp
pumpkin pie spice 1/2 tsp

Directions

Prepare the Batter: Preheat the oven to 350°F (175°C). Line a cupcake tin with 12 liners. Mix flour, baking powder, baking soda, pumpkin pie spice, and salt in a large bowl.

Mix *Wet Ingredients:* In another bowl, combine pumpkin puree, maple syrup, almond milk, melted coconut oil, and vanilla extract. Stir until smooth.

Combine: Gradually add the wet and dry ingredients, stirring gently until combined. Avoid overmixing to keep the cupcakes light.

Bake: Divide the batter evenly among the cupcake liners. Bake for 20–25 minutes or until a toothpick inserted in the center comes clean. Let cool completely on a wire rack.

Prepare the Frosting: Whip chilled coconut cream with maple syrup and pumpkin pie spice until fluffy. Spread or pipe onto cooled cupcakes.

Serve: Garnish with a sprinkle of cinnamon or chopped nuts for added texture and flavor.

Nutritional Info (Per Serving)

Calories: 180 | Protein: 3g | Carbs: 16g | Fats: 13g
Fiber: 4g | Cholesterol: 0mg | Sodium: 180mg | Potassium: 350mg

Raspberry Chia Jam Thumbprint Cookies

Prep. time: 20 min   Cook time: 15 min   Serves: 12
                          Chill Time: 20 minutes

Ingredients

Chia Jam
raspberries 1 cup, fresh or frozen
Maple syrup 1 tbsp
chia seeds 1 tbsp
Cookies
almond flour 1 1/4 cups
Coconut oil 3 tbsp, melted.
Maple syrup 3 tbsp
vanilla extract 1/2 tsp
salt 1/8 tsp

Directions

Prepare Chia Jam: In a small saucepan over medium heat, cook raspberries until softened, about 5 minutes. Mash with a fork and stir in chia seeds and maple syrup. Remove from heat and let cool, allowing it to thicken.

Make Cookie Dough: In a medium bowl, mix almond flour, melted coconut oil, maple syrup, vanilla extract, and salt until a soft dough forms. Chill the dough for 20 minutes to firm it up.

Shape Cookies: Preheat the oven to 350°F (175°C). Line a baking sheet with parchment paper. Roll the dough into 12 equal balls and place on the baking sheet. Press your thumb into the center of each ball to create a well.

Fill and Bake: Fill each well with a small spoonful of chia jam. Bake for 12–15 minutes or until the edges are lightly golden. Cool completely on the baking sheet.

Serve: Enjoy as is or with a light dusting of powdered coconut sugar for extra sweetness.

Nutritional Info (Per Serving)

Calories: 180 | Protein: 3g | Carbs: 16g | Fats: 13g
Fiber: 4g | Cholesterol: 0mg | Sodium: 60mg | Potassium: 150mg

Chapter 8: Sauces, Dips, and Essentials

Creamy Cashew Alfredo Sauce

Prep. time: 10 min

Cook time: 5 min
Soaking Time: 2 hours

Serves: 4

Ingredients

raw cashews 1 cup, soaked for 2 hours or boiled for 10 minutes
unsweetened plant-based milk 1 cup (e.g., almond or oat milk)
nutritional yeast 3 tbsp
garlic cloves 2, minced
lemon juice 2 tbsp
salt 1/2 tsp
black pepper 1/4 tsp
optional: pinch of nutmeg or red pepper flakes for added flavor

Directions

Soak Cashews: Soak cashews in water for 2 hours or boil for 10 minutes to soften. Drain and rinse thoroughly.

Blend Ingredients: Add soaked cashews, plant-based milk, nutritional yeast, garlic, lemon juice, salt, and pepper to a high-speed blender. Blend until completely smooth, scraping down the sides as needed. Adjust consistency with more milk if necessary.

Heat Sauce: Transfer the blended sauce to a saucepan over low heat. Warm gently while stirring until heated through. Do not boil to prevent curdling.

Serve: Toss with cooked pasta and roasted vegetables or use as a creamy sauce for casseroles.

Optional Toppings: Sprinkle with fresh parsley, vegan parmesan, or crushed walnuts for added texture and flavor.

Nutritional Info (Per Serving)

Calories: 180 | Protein: 6g | Carbs: 10g | Fats: 13g
Fiber: 2g | Cholesterol: 0mg | Sodium: 250mg | Potassium: 300mg

Smoky Chipotle Mayo (Dairy-Free)

Prep. time: 5 min

Setting time: 30 min

Serves: 6

Ingredients

unsweetened plant-based mayonnaise 1/2 cup
Chipotle pepper in adobo sauce: 1 to 2 peppers, finely chopped (adjust to desired spice level)
adobo sauce 1 tbsp
lime juice 1 tbsp
garlic powder 1/2 tsp
smoked paprika 1/2 tsp
salt 1/4 tsp
black pepper 1/4 tsp

Directions

Blend Ingredients: In a small bowl or jar, combine plant-based mayonnaise, chopped chipotle pepper, adobo sauce, lime juice, garlic powder, smoked paprika, salt, and black pepper.

Mix Well: Stir or whisk until all ingredients are fully incorporated and the sauce is smooth.

Chill (Optional): For a deeper flavor, cover and let the mayo sit in the fridge for at least 30 minutes to allow the flavors to meld.

Serve: Use as a dip, sandwich spread, or drizzle over roasted veggies, tacos, or burgers for a smoky, spicy kick.

Optional Variations:

Add a teaspoon of maple syrup for a sweet-spicy balance.

Blend in a small handful of cilantro for extra freshness.

Nutritional Info (Per Serving)

Calories: 70 | Protein: 1g | Carbs: 3g | Fats: 6g
Fiber: 1g | Cholesterol: 0mg | Sodium: 250mg | Potassium: 50mg

Classic Vegan Basil Pesto

Prep. time: 10 min   Total time: 10 min   Serves: 6

Ingredients

fresh basil leaves 2 cups, packed
Pine nuts 1/4 cup (or use walnuts for a more affordable option)
garlic two cloves
nutritional yeast 2 tbsp
lemon juice 1 tbsp
extra virgin olive oil 1/3 cup
salt 1/4 tsp
black pepper 1/4 tsp

Directions

Prepare Ingredients: Wash and dry the fresh basil leaves. Peel the garlic cloves.
Blend: In a food processor or blender, combine the basil, pine nuts, garlic, nutritional yeast, lemon juice, salt, and black pepper. Pulse until the ingredients are coarsely chopped.
Add Olive Oil: Slowly stream in the olive oil while blending until the pesto reaches a smooth, creamy consistency.
Adjust Flavor: Taste and add more salt, pepper, or lemon juice if desired.
Serve: Toss the pesto with your favorite pasta, spread it on sandwiches, or use it as a dip.
Optional Variations:
Add a handful of spinach or arugula for extra greens.
Substitute sunflower or pumpkin seeds for the pine nuts for a nut-free version.

Nutritional Info (Per Serving)
Calories: 180 | Protein: 3g | Carbs: 5g | Fats: 17g
Fiber: 2g | Cholesterol: 0mg | Sodium: 250mg | Potassium: 200mg

Savory Tahini Miso Dressing

Prep. time: 5 min   Total time: 5 min   Serves: 6

Ingredients

tahini 1/4 cup
white miso paste 2 tbsp
rice vinegar 1 tbsp
Maple syrup 1 tsp
lemon juice 1 tbsp
Water 2-3 tbsp (adjust for desired consistency)
garlic, one clove, minced
sesame oil 1 tsp (optional for added depth)
sesame seeds (optional for garnish)

Directions

Prepare Ingredients: Mince the garlic and juice the lemon.
Mix Dressing: In a small bowl, combine tahini, white miso paste, rice vinegar, maple syrup, lemon juice, and minced garlic.
Adjust Consistency: Gradually add water, stirring until the dressing reaches a smooth, pourable consistency. You can adjust the water based on how thick or thin you prefer the dressing.
Taste and Adjust: Taste the dressing and add more miso or lemon juice if needed. For extra depth, add sesame oil.
Serve: Drizzle the dressing over salads, roasted vegetables, or grain bowls. Garnish with sesame seeds if desired.
Optional Variations:
Add a small piece of fresh ginger for an extra zing.
Use a splash of tamari or soy sauce for an umami flavor.

Nutritional Info (Per Serving)
Calories: 180 | Protein: 4g | Carbs: 7g | Fats: 15g
Fiber: 2g | Cholesterol: 0mg | Sodium: 520mg | Potassium: 170mg

Sweet and Tangy Mango Salsa

Prep. time: 10 min   Total time: 10 min   Serves: 4

Ingredients

mango, diced one large
red bell pepper, finely chopped 1/2
red onion, finely chopped 1/4
cucumber, diced 1/2
Fresh cilantro, chopped 2 tbsp.
lime juice 1 tbsp
maple syrup or agave syrup 1 tsp
salt 1/4 tsp
black pepper 1/4 tsp
jalapeño (optional), finely chopped 1

Directions

Prepare Ingredients: Dice the mango, red bell pepper, cucumber, and onion into small pieces. Chop the cilantro and, if using, finely chop the jalapeño.

Combine: In a medium bowl, combine the diced mango, red bell pepper, cucumber, onion, cilantro, and jalapeño.

Add Flavor: Squeeze the lime juice over the salsa and drizzle in the maple syrup. Sprinkle with salt and black pepper and stir everything together until well-mixed.

Taste and Adjust: Taste the salsa and adjust the seasoning as needed. If you prefer a sweeter salsa, add a bit of maple syrup.

Serve: Serve immediately with tortilla chips, tacos, or as a topping for salads or grilled vegetables.

Optional Variations:

Add a small handful of pomegranate seeds for extra crunch and a burst of color. Replace the maple syrup with a pinch of cumin or smoked paprika for a savorier version.

Nutritional Info (Per Serving)

Calories: 60 | Protein: 1g | Carbs: 16g | Fats: 0g
Fiber: 2g | Cholesterol: 0mg | Sodium: 120mg | Potassium: 260mg

5-Minute Garlic Hummus

Prep. time: 5 min   Total time: 5 min   Serves: 4

Ingredients

chickpeas (canned or cooked), drained and rinsed one can (15 oz)
tahini 1/4 cup
garlic cloves, minced 2
fresh lemon juice 2 tbsp
olive oil 1 tbsp
ground cumin 1/2 tsp
sea salt 1/4 tsp
black pepper 1/4 tsp
Water 2-4 tbsp (adjust for desired consistency)

Directions

Prepare ingredients: Drain and rinse the chickpeas if canned. Peel and mince the garlic cloves.

Blend: In a food processor, combine the chickpeas, tahini, minced garlic, lemon juice, olive oil, cumin, salt, and pepper.

Process: Blend until smooth, adding water a tablespoon at a time to achieve your desired consistency. Continue processing until the hummus is creamy.

Taste and Adjust: Taste the hummus and adjust the seasoning as needed by adding more salt, garlic, or lemon juice for extra flavor.

Serve: Transfer the hummus to a serving bowl and drizzle with extra olive oil. Garnish with paprika or fresh parsley.

Optional Toppings and Variations:

Top with toasted pine nuts for extra texture.
Add roasted red peppers or sun-dried tomatoes for a unique twist.

Nutritional Info (Per Serving)

Calories: 120 | Protein: 5g | Carbs: 16g | Fats: 6g
Fiber: 4g | Cholesterol: 0mg | Sodium: 240mg | Potassium: 230mg

Dairy-Free Ranch Dressing

Prep. time: 5 min   Total time: 5 min   Serves: 6

Ingredients

unsweetened plant-based milk (such as almond or soy) 1/4 cup
tahini 2 tbsp
apple cider vinegar 1 tbsp
fresh lemon juice 1 tbsp
garlic powder 1/2 tsp
onion powder 1/2 tsp
dried dill 1 tsp
sea salt 1/4 tsp
black pepper 1/4 tsp
optional: chopped fresh parsley for garnish

Directions

Blend Ingredients: In a blender or food processor, combine the plant-based milk, tahini, apple cider vinegar, lemon juice, garlic powder, onion powder, dried dill, salt, and pepper.

Process: Blend until smooth and creamy. If the dressing is too thick, add a tablespoon of water until the desired consistency is achieved.

Taste and Adjust: Taste the dressing and adjust the seasonings if necessary, adding more salt, lemon juice, or dill for extra flavor.

Serve: Pour the ranch dressing into a serving bowl and sprinkle with freshly chopped parsley if desired.

Optional Variations:
Add a teaspoon of nutritional yeast for a cheesy flavor.
Include a dash of hot sauce or cayenne pepper for a spicier kick.

Nutritional Info (Per Serving)

Calories: 80 | Protein: 2g | Carbs: 3g | Fats: 6g
Fiber: 1g | Cholesterol: 0mg | Sodium: 180mg | Potassium: 50mg

Spicy Peanut Sauce for Noodles and Veggies

Prep. time: 5 min   Total time: 5 min   Serves: 4

Ingredients

peanut butter 1/4 cup
soy sauce (or tamari for gluten-free) 2 tbsp
rice vinegar 1 tbsp
sesame oil 1 tbsp
Maple syrup 1 tbsp
Sriracha sauce (or chili paste) 1 tsp (adjust for desired heat)
garlic powder 1/2 tsp
fresh lime juice 1 tsp
water (to thin the sauce) 2-4 tbsp

Directions

Mix Ingredients: In a bowl, whisk together peanut butter, soy sauce, rice vinegar, sesame oil, maple syrup, sriracha, garlic powder, and lime juice until smooth.

Thin Sauce: Gradually add water, one tablespoon at a time, until the sauce reaches your desired consistency for noodles or veggie coating.

Taste and Adjust: Taste the sauce and add more sriracha for heat, maple syrup for sweetness, or soy sauce for saltiness.

Serve: Pour the sauce over cooked noodles or roasted/steamed veggies and toss to coat evenly. Garnish with chopped cilantro, sesame seeds, or green onions for extra flavor.

Optional Variations:
Add grated ginger for a fresh, zesty twist.
For extra crunch, top with crushed peanuts.
This spicy peanut sauce adds a rich, flavorful kick to noodles, steamed veggies, or rice bowls!

Nutritional Info (Per Serving)

Calories: 150 | Protein: 5g | Carbs: 8g | Fats: 12g
Fiber: 2g | Cholesterol: 0mg | Sodium: 300mg | Potassium: 150mg

Vegan Parmesan Sprinkle

Prep. time: 5 min   Total time: 5 min   Serves: 5

Ingredients

raw cashews 1/2 cup
nutritional yeast 1/4 cup
garlic powder 1 tsp
onion powder 1/2 tsp
lemon zest 1 tsp
salt 1/2 tsp
black pepper 1/4 tsp

Directions

Blend Ingredients: Place the raw cashews, nutritional yeast, garlic powder, onion powder, lemon zest, salt, and black pepper in a high-speed blender or food processor. Pulse until finely ground; the mixture resembles a crumbly, parmesan-like texture.
Taste and Adjust: Taste the sprinkle and adjust the seasoning. Add more lemon zest or nutritional yeast if you prefer a tangier flavor.
Store: Transfer the vegan parmesan sprinkle into an airtight container and store it in the refrigerator for up to 2 weeks.
Serve: Sprinkle on pasta, salads, roasted veggies, or soups for a flavorful, plant-based alternative to traditional parmesan cheese.
Optional Variations:
Add dried basil or oregano for a herby twist.
For a richer flavor, try adding a pinch of smoked paprika.

Nutritional Info (Per Serving)
Calories: 80 | Protein: 3g | Carbs: 4g | Fats: 6g
Fiber: 1g | Cholesterol: 0mg | Sodium: 250mg | Potassium: 150mg

Easy Coconut Milk Curry Base

Prep. time: 10 min   Cook time: 20 min   Serves: 4

Ingredients

coconut oil 1 tbsp
yellow onion 1, diced
garlic cloves 3, minced
fresh ginger 1-inch piece, grated
curry powder 1 tbsp
ground turmeric 1 tsp
cumin 1 tsp
coriander 1 tsp
coconut milk (full-fat) 1 can (13.5 oz)
vegetable broth 1 cup
tomato paste 2 tbsp
salt 1/2 tsp
black pepper 1/4 tsp
lime juice 1 tbsp

Directions

Cook Aromatics: Heat the coconut oil in a large pan over medium heat. Add the diced onion and cook until softened about 5 minutes. Add the minced garlic and grated ginger and cook for another 2 minutes until fragrant.
Add Spices: Stir in the curry powder, ground turmeric, cumin, and coriander, and cook for 1 minute to toast the spices.
Add Liquids: Pour in the coconut milk, vegetable broth, and tomato paste, and stir well to combine. Bring the mixture to a simmer.
Simmer: Let the curry base simmer for 15 minutes, stirring occasionally, until it thickens slightly—season with salt, black pepper, and lime juice, and taste for seasoning adjustments.
Serve the curry base over rice, quinoa, or your favorite vegetables. For a protein boost, add tofu, chickpeas, or tempeh.
Optional Toppings:
Fresh cilantro
Chopped peanuts or cashews for crunch
A drizzle of additional coconut milk for extra creaminess

Nutritional Info (Per Serving)
Calories: 180 | Protein: 3g | Carbs: 16g | Fats: 13g
Fiber: 4g | Cholesterol: 0mg | Sodium: 600mg | Potassium: 550mg

Zesty Lemon and Herb Vinaigrette

Prep. time: 10 min   Total time: 10 min   Serves: 6

Ingredients

fresh lemon juice 1/4 cup
extra virgin olive oil 1/2 cup
Dijon mustard one tablespoon
maple syrup, one teaspoon
Garlic minced one clove.
fresh parsley finely chopped two tablespoons
fresh dill finely chopped one tablespoon
fresh oregano finely chopped one tablespoon
sea salt 1/2 teaspoon
Black pepper freshly ground 1/4 teaspoon.

Directions

Combine Liquids: In a small bowl or jar, combine the lemon juice, olive oil, Dijon mustard, and maple syrup. Whisk or shake the jar vigorously until the ingredients are emulsified.

Add Aromatics and Herbs: Stir in the minced garlic, parsley, dill, and oregano. Season with sea salt and black pepper, adjusting the amounts to taste.

Rest and Infuse: Let the vinaigrette rest for 5 minutes to let the flavors meld and the herbs infuse into the liquid.

Adjust Seasoning: Taste the vinaigrette and add more lemon juice, salt, or herbs as desired for balance.

Serve: Use immediately as a dressing for salads, roasted vegetables, or grain bowls. This vinaigrette can also serve as a flavorful marinade for tofu, tempeh, or grilled vegetables.

Optional Variations

Add tahini for creaminess.
Incorporate nutritional yeast for a cheesy flavor.
Substitute lime juice for lemon for a tangy twist.

Nutritional Information (Per Serving):

Calories: 180 | Protein: 1g | Carbs: 3g | Fats: 18g
Fiber: 1g | Cholesterol: 0mg | Sodium: 200mg | Potassium: 50mg

Roasted Red Pepper Cashew Dip

Prep. time: 10 min   Setting time: 30 min   Serves: 6 (soaking cashews)

Ingredients

raw cashews 1 cup
Roasted red peppers drained 1 cup.
garlic clove, one large
lemon juice, two tablespoons
nutritional yeast two tablespoons
smoked paprika, one teaspoon
sea salt 1/2 teaspoon
olive oil one tablespoon
water 2-4 tablespoons

Directions

Soak Cashews: Place cashews in a bowl and cover with hot water. Let them soak for 30 minutes to soften. Drain and rinse thoroughly.

Prepare Ingredients: Add the soaked cashews, roasted red peppers, garlic, lemon juice, nutritional yeast, smoked paprika, and sea salt to a high-speed blender or food processor.

Blend Ingredients: Begin blending the mixture, slowly adding one tablespoon of water at a time to achieve a creamy and smooth consistency. Scrape down the sides as needed to ensure all ingredients are incorporated.

Adjust Seasoning: Taste the dip and add more salt, lemon juice, or paprika to suit your preference.

Add Olive Oil: Blend in olive oil for a richer texture and enhanced flavor.

Serve: Serve immediately as a dip for vegetables, crackers, or pita bread. This dip can also be used as a spread for sandwiches or wraps.

Optional Variations

Add roasted garlic for a sweeter, deeper flavor.
Incorporate a pinch of cayenne for a spicy kick.
Mix in fresh basil for a herby twist.

Nutritional Information (Per Serving):

Calories: 180 | Protein: 5g | Carbs: 11g | Fats: 13g
Fiber: 2g | Cholesterol: 0mg | Sodium: 260mg | Potassium: 350mg

Creamy Avocado Cilantro Lime Dressing

Prep. time: 10 min   Total time: 10 min   Serves: 6

Ingredients

ripe avocado, one large
Fresh cilantro leaves chopped 1/2 cup.
lime juice, three tablespoons
olive oil two tablespoons
unsweetened almond milk 1/4 cup
garlic clove, one large
jalapeño seeded (optional) 1 small
sea salt 1/2 teaspoon
black pepper freshly ground 1/4 teaspoon

Directions

Prepare Ingredients: Scoop the avocado flesh into a blender or food processor. Add chopped cilantro, lime juice, olive oil, almond milk, garlic, and jalapeño.
Blend Ingredients: Blend until smooth and creamy, scraping down the sides of the blender as needed. Adjust the consistency by adding more almond milk, one tablespoon at a time, if a thinner dressing is desired.
Season and Taste: Add Sea salt and black pepper. Blend briefly and taste to adjust seasoning as needed.
Serve: Use immediately as a salad dressing, a veggie dip, or a drizzle over grain bowls and tacos.
Optional Variations
Add a teaspoon of maple syrup for a touch of sweetness.
Incorporate a pinch of cumin for an earthy flavor.
Swap lime juice with lemon juice for a different citrus note.

Nutritional Information (Per Serving):

Calories: 180 | Protein: 2g | Carbs: 7g | Fats: 16g
Fiber: 5g | Cholesterol: 0mg | Sodium: 120mg | Potassium: 450mg

Balsamic Glaze for Roasted Vegetables and Salads

Prep. time: 5 min   Setting Time: 10 minutes   Serves: 6
                           (cooling time)

Ingredients

balsamic vinegar 1 cup
Maple syrup two tablespoons

Directions

Combine Ingredients: Add balsamic vinegar and maple syrup to a small saucepan over medium heat.
Simmer and Reduce: Bring the mixture to a gentle simmer, stirring occasionally. Lower the heat and let it reduce for 10-15 minutes until the liquid thickens slightly and coats the back of a spoon.
Cool: Remove the pan from heat and allow the glaze to cool. The glaze will thicken further as it cools.
Serve: Drizzle over roasted vegetables, salads, or grain bowls. Store any leftovers in an airtight container in the refrigerator for up to two weeks.
Optional Variations
Add a pinch of sea salt for a savory note.
Incorporate a teaspoon of minced garlic or fresh rosemary for a herby flavor.
Mix in a dash of cayenne for a subtle spicy kick.

Nutritional Information (Per Serving):

Calories: 60 | Protein: 0g | Carbs: 14g | Fats: 0g
Fiber: 0g | Cholesterol: 0mg | Sodium: 10mg | Potassium: 90mg

Chapter 9: Plant-Based Milk and Yogurt

Almond Breeze Classic Almond Milk Made Easy

Prep. time: 10 min   Setting Time: 8 hours (soaking   Serves: 4
almonds)

Ingredients

raw almonds 1 cup
water for soaking 2 cups
filtered water 4 cups
maple syrup or agave one tablespoon (optional)
vanilla extract one teaspoon (optional)
sea salt pinch
Optional Variations
Add cocoa powder for a chocolate almond milk
version.
Blend with a pinch of cinnamon or cardamom for
a spiced flavor.
Use dates instead of maple syrup for natural
sweetness.

Directions

Soak Almonds: Place raw almonds in a bowl and cover with water. Let them soak for at least 8 hours or overnight to soften. Drain and rinse thoroughly.

Blend Ingredients: Add the soaked almonds and filtered water to a high-speed blender. Blend high for 1-2 minutes until the mixture is creamy and the almonds are finely ground.

Strain Milk: Pour the mixture through a nut milk bag or cheesecloth into a bowl, squeezing gently to extract all the liquid. Discard or save the almond pulp for other recipes.

Sweeten and Flavor: Pour the strained almond milk back into the blender. Add maple syrup or agave, vanilla extract, and a pinch of sea salt if desired. Blend briefly to combine.

Serve: Transfer the almond milk to a glass container and refrigerate for up to 4 days. Shake well before serving.

Serving Suggestions

Serve chilled as a refreshing drink. You can also use it in smoothies, coffee, or cereal. Pair it with baked goods or enjoy it on its own.

Nutritional Information (Per Serving):

Calories: 80 | Protein: 2g | Carbs: 2g | Fats: 7g
Fiber: 1g | Cholesterol: 0mg | Sodium: 50mg | Potassium: 150mg

Oat's the Way Creamy Homemade Oat Milk

Prep. time: 5 min   Cook time: min   Serves: 4

Ingredients

rolled oats 1 cup
filtered water 4 cups
maple syrup or agave one tablespoon (optional)
vanilla extract one teaspoon (optional)
sea salt pinch
Optional Variations
Add a pinch of cinnamon for warmth.
Blend with cocoa powder for a chocolate version.
Incorporate soaked dates instead of syrup for
natural sweetness.

Directions

Combine Ingredients: Add rolled oats and filtered water to a high-speed blender. Blend on high for 30-40 seconds. Avoid over-blending to prevent sliminess.

Strain Milk: Pour the mixture into a bowl through a fine-mesh sieve, nut milk bag, or cheesecloth. Strain thoroughly, discarding or saving the oat pulp for baking or other recipes.

Sweeten and Flavor: Pour the strained oat milk back into the blender. Add maple syrup or agave, vanilla extract, and a pinch of sea salt if desired. Blend briefly to combine.

Serve: Transfer the oat milk to a glass container and refrigerate for up to 4 days. Shake well before serving.

Serving Suggestions

Enjoy as a refreshing drink, in smoothies, with coffee, or over cereal.

Nutritional Information (Per Serving):

Calories: 120 | Protein: 3g | Carbs: 14g | Fats: 2g
Fiber: 2g | Cholesterol: 0mg | Sodium: 50mg | Potassium: 100mg

Cashew Bliss Velvety Cashew Milk with a Hint of Vanilla

Prep. time: 5 min

Setting Time: 2-4 hours
(soaking cashews)

Serves: 4

Ingredients

raw cashews 1 cup
filtered water 4 cups
maple syrup or agave one tablespoon (optional)
vanilla extract one teaspoon
sea salt pinch

Optional Variations

Add cinnamon or nutmeg for a spiced version.
Blend with one tablespoon of cocoa powder for chocolate cashew milk.
Incorporate a teaspoon of almond or coconut extract for a unique twist.

Directions

Soak Cashews: Place cashews in a bowl and cover with water. Soak for 2-4 hours to soften. Drain and rinse thoroughly.

Blend Ingredients: Add soaked cashews, filtered water, maple syrup or agave (if using), vanilla extract, and a pinch of sea salt to a high-speed blender. Blend on high for 1-2 minutes until smooth and creamy.

Strain Milk (Optional): If you prefer a smoother texture, pour the milk through a nut milk bag or fine-mesh sieve into a bowl.

Serve: Transfer the cashew milk to a glass container and refrigerate for up to 4 days. Shake well before serving.

Serving Suggestions

Enjoy chilled as a drink, in coffee, or poured over granola. It can also be used in smoothies or as a creamy base for soups and sauces.

Nutritional Information (Per Serving):

Calories: 160 | Protein: 5g | Carbs: 8g | Fats: 12g
Fiber: 1g | Cholesterol: 0mg | Sodium: 50mg | Potassium: 200mg

Coconut Dreams Rich Coconut Milk for Cooking or Sipping

Prep. time: 5 min

Total time: 5 min

Serves: 4 cups

Ingredients

unsweetened shredded coconut 2 cups
hot water 4 cups
maple syrup or agave one tablespoon (optional)
vanilla extract one teaspoon (optional)
sea salt pinch

Optional Variations

Add a pinch of cinnamon or nutmeg for a warm spice note.
Blend with cocoa powder for a chocolate coconut milk version.

Directions

Blend Ingredients: Add shredded coconut and hot water to a high-speed blender. Blend on high for 2-3 minutes until the mixture is creamy and well combined.

Strain Milk: Pour the mixture through a nut milk bag, cheesecloth, or fine-mesh sieve into a bowl, squeezing out as much liquid as possible. Reserve the coconut pulp for other recipes.

Sweeten and Flavor: Pour the strained coconut milk back into the blender. Add maple syrup or agave, vanilla extract, and a pinch of sea salt if desired. Blend briefly to combine.

Serve: Transfer the coconut milk to a glass container and refrigerate for 5 days. Shake well before using, as separation is natural.

Serving Suggestions

Use as a base for soups, curries, or sauces. Enjoy as a creamy beverage, in coffee, or as a smoothie base.

Nutritional Information (Per Serving):

Calories: 180 | Protein: 2g | Carbs: 5g | Fats: 18g
Fiber: 3g | Cholesterol: 0mg | Sodium: 20mg | Potassium: 250mg

Soy Simple Protein-Packed Soy Milk for All Occasions

Prep. time: 10 min   Setting Time: 12 hours (soaking   Serves: 4 cups
                          soybeans)

Ingredients

dry soybeans 1 cup
filtered water 4 cups for blending
maple syrup or agave one tablespoon (optional)
vanilla extract one teaspoon (optional)
sea salt pinch
Optional Variations
Add cocoa powder for chocolate soy milk.
Incorporate soaked dates instead of syrup for
natural sweetness.
Blend with a pinch of cinnamon or turmeric for a
spiced twist.

Directions

Soak Soybeans: Rinse the soybeans and place them in a bowl. Cover with water and soak for 12 hours or overnight. Drain and rinse thoroughly.
Cook Soybeans: Soak the soybeans in fresh water for 20-25 minutes to remove any bitter taste. Drain and let cool slightly.
Blend Ingredients: Add cooked soybeans and 4 cups of filtered water to a high-speed blender. Blend on high for 2 minutes until smooth.
Strain Milk: Pour the blended mixture through a nut milk bag or cheesecloth into a bowl, squeezing out as much liquid as possible. Discard or save the soy pulp for other uses.
Sweeten and Flavor: Pour the strained soy milk back into the blender. Add maple syrup or agave, vanilla extract, and a pinch of sea salt if desired. Blend briefly to combine.
Serve: Transfer the soy milk to a glass container and refrigerate for 5 days. Shake well before serving.

Serving Suggestions

Enjoy as a protein-rich beverage, in coffee, or over cereal. Use soy milk for added creaminess in baking, soups, or smoothies.

Nutritional Information (Per Serving):

Calories: 140 | Protein: 7g | Carbs: 6g | Fats: 6g
Fiber: 2g | Cholesterol: 0mg | Sodium: 50mg | Potassium: 300mg

Hemp Harmony Nutty Hemp Milk with Omega Boost

Prep. time: 5 min   Total time: 5 min   Serves: 4 cups

Ingredients

hemp seeds 1/2 cup
filtered water 4 cups
maple syrup or agave one tablespoon (optional)
vanilla extract one teaspoon (optional)
sea salt pinch
Optional Variations
Add a pinch of cinnamon for warmth.
Blend with cocoa powder for chocolate hemp
milk.
Incorporate soaked dates for a natural sweetness.

Directions

Blend Ingredients: Add hemp seeds and filtered water to a high-speed blender. Blend on high for 1-2 minutes until smooth and creamy.
Strain Milk (Optional): If desired, strain the mixture through a nut milk bag or fine-mesh sieve to remove any remaining pulp.
Sweeten and Flavor: Return the strained milk to the blender and add maple syrup or agave, vanilla extract, and a pinch of sea salt (optional). Blend briefly to combine.
Serve: Transfer the hemp milk to a glass container and refrigerate for 5 days. Shake well before serving.

Serving Suggestions

Enjoy it as a refreshing beverage, in smoothies, over granola, or in coffee. For a plant-based milk alternative, use it in baking or cooking.

Nutritional Information (Per Serving):

Calories: 180 | Protein: 7g | Carbs: 4g | Fats: 15g
Fiber: 2g | Cholesterol: 0mg | Sodium: 40mg | Potassium: 350mg

Golden Glow Milk Turmeric-Infused Plant-Based Latte Base

Prep. time: 5 min   Total time: min   Serves: 4 cups

Ingredients

unsweetened almond milk 2 cups
coconut milk (full-fat or light) 1 cup
ground turmeric 1 1/2 teaspoons
ground cinnamon 1/2 teaspoon
fresh ginger (grated) 1 teaspoon
maple syrup or agave one tablespoon (optional)
vanilla extract one teaspoon
black pepper pinch (to enhance turmeric
absorption)

Directions

Heat Milk: combine almond milk and coconut milk in a small saucepan. Warm over medium heat, stirring occasionally, until hot but not boiling.

Add Spices: Stir in turmeric, cinnamon, grated ginger, maple syrup, vanilla extract, and a pinch of black pepper. Stir until all ingredients are well combined.

Simmer: Reduce the heat and let the mixture simmer for 3-4 minutes, allowing the flavors to meld.

Optional Variations

For a creamier texture, increase the amount of coconut milk.

Blend in a scoop of plant-based protein powder for added nutrition.

Top with a sprinkle of cinnamon or a dash of cayenne pepper for an extra kick.

For a sweeter taste, increase the maple syrup to 2 tablespoons.

Add a splash of almond extract for a deeper flavor.

Serve: Remove from heat and pour into mugs. Enjoy the Golden Glow Milk as a latte base, or add more milk for a lighter drink.

Nutritional Information (Per Serving):

Calories: 180 | Protein: 3g | Carbs: 16g | Fats: 13g
Fiber: 4g | Cholesterol: 0mg | Sodium: 100mg | Potassium: 450mg

Tangy Delight Basic Coconut Yogurt with Probiotics

Prep. time: 10 min   *Setting Time:* 24 hours   Serves: 4

Ingredients

canned full-fat coconut milk two cans (13.5 oz each)
probiotic capsules (or powder) 2 capsules
maple syrup or agave one tablespoon (optional, for sweetness)
vanilla extract one teaspoon (optional)
lemon juice one tablespoon (for tang)

Optional Variations

Add a splash of coconut water for a thinner consistency.

For a sweeter taste, increase the maple syrup or agave.

Blend in some fresh fruit puree (e.g., mango or berries) after the yogurt has set for added flavor and nutrition.

Top with granola, chia seeds, or fresh fruit for extra texture and nutrients.

Directions

Prepare Coconut Milk: Shake the cans of coconut milk before opening to ensure the coconut cream is well-mixed. Pour the coconut milk into a clean glass jar or bowl.

Add Probiotics: Open the probiotic capsules and sprinkle the powder into the coconut milk. Stir gently to combine. If using probiotic powder, follow the instructions on the package for the right amount.

Add Sweetener and Flavor: Add maple syrup or agave (if using), vanilla extract, and lemon juice. Stir until well combined.

Set Yogurt: Cover the jar or bowl with a clean cloth or lid. Let the coconut milk mixture sit at room temperature (ideally around 75°F/24°C) for 24 hours to ferment. After 12 hours, check the yogurt to see if it has thickened and developed the desired tang. If it's too thin, allow it to sit longer.

Serve: After fermenting the yogurt, store it in the refrigerator for 4-6 hours to cool and firm up. Serve chilled with toppings such as granola, fresh berries, or a drizzle of honey.

Nutritional Information (Per Serving):

Calories: 180 | Protein: 3g | Carbs: 16g | Fats: 13g
Fiber: 4g | Cholesterol: 0mg | Sodium: 600mg | Potassium: 550mg

Berry Bliss Yogurt Quick Mixed-Berry Coconut Yogurt

Prep. time: 10 min   Total time: 10 min   Serves: 4

Ingredients

canned full-fat coconut milk one can (13.5 oz)
frozen mixed berries 1 1/2 cups
unsweetened coconut yogurt 1/2 cup
maple syrup or agave one tablespoon (optional for sweetness)
vanilla extract one teaspoon
chia seeds one tablespoon (optional for extra fiber)
fresh berries for topping (optional)
Optional Variations
For a thicker yogurt, increase the amount of coconut yogurt.
Add a handful of spinach or kale and blend it for a green berry yogurt.
For a protein boost, mix in a scoop of plant-based protein powder.
Top with granola, shredded coconut, or almond butter for extra texture.

Directions

Blend Coconut Yogurt: In a blender, combine the coconut milk, mixed berries, coconut yogurt, maple syrup (if using), and vanilla extract. Blend until smooth and creamy.

Add Chia Seeds: If you want extra fiber, add chia seeds to the blender and pulse for a few seconds. The chia seeds will thicken the yogurt slightly.

Taste and Adjust: Taste the yogurt and adjust the sweetness, if necessary, by adding more maple syrup or agave. Add more coconut milk or water and blend again if you prefer a thinner consistency.

Serve: Spoon the mixed berry coconut yogurt into bowls or cups. Top with fresh berries, granola, or any additional toppings you prefer.

Nutritional Information (Per Serving):

Calories: 180 | Protein: 3g | Carbs: 16g | Fats: 13g
Fiber: 4g | Cholesterol: 0mg | Sodium: 20mg | Potassium: 400mg

Vanilla Maple Yogurt Sweet and Creamy Cashew-Based Treat

Prep. time: 15 min   Setting Time: 4-6 hours (or overnight)   Serves: 4

Ingredients

raw cashews (soaked for 4 hours) 1 cup
unsweetened almond milk 1/2 cup
Maple syrup three tablespoons
vanilla extract one teaspoon
lemon juice, one tablespoon
coconut yogurt (optional, for extra creaminess) 1/4 cup
pinch of sea salt
Optional Variations
For a thicker texture, increase the amount of coconut yogurt.
Add one tablespoon of chia seeds for an extra fiber boost.
Top with fresh fruit like berries, bananas, or a sprinkle of cinnamon.
For a richer taste, mix in 1 tablespoon of coconut oil.

Directions

Soak Cashews: Soak the raw cashews in water for at least 4 hours or overnight. Drain and rinse before using.

Blend Ingredients: In a high-speed blender, combine soaked cashews, almond milk, maple syrup, vanilla extract, lemon juice, and coconut yogurt (if using). Blend until smooth and creamy.

Taste and Adjust: Taste the mixture and adjust sweetness if needed by adding more maple syrup. If the consistency is too thick, add more almond milk to reach the desired texture.

Refrigerate: Transfer the cashew yogurt mixture to a bowl or jars and refrigerate for 4-6 hours, or overnight, to allow it to set and thicken.

Serve: Once set, scoop the yogurt into bowls. Top with fresh fruit, nuts, or granola for added texture.

Nutritional Information (Per Serving):

Calories: 180 | Protein: 4g | Carbs: 16g | Fats: 12g
Fiber: 3g | Cholesterol: 0mg | Sodium: 40mg | Potassium: 210mg

Chapter 10: Homemade Meat and Cheese Alternatives

Hearty Lentil Loaf: a Perfect Plant-Based Meatloaf

Prep. time: 15 min   Cook time: 45 min   Serves: 6

Ingredients

green or brown lentils (cooked and drained) 1 1/2 cups

rolled oats 1/2 cup

chopped onion 1/2 cup

garlic (minced) 2 cloves

carrot (grated) 1 medium

celery (chopped) 1 stalk

tomato paste two tablespoons

flaxseed meal (for egg replacement): 1 tablespoon

water three tablespoons

soy sauce or tamari, one tablespoon

olive oil one tablespoon

ground cumin 1/2 teaspoon

ground coriander 1/2 teaspoon

salt 1/2 teaspoon

black pepper 1/4 teaspoon

Optional Toppings

tomato ketchup or BBQ sauce 2-3 tablespoons

fresh parsley (chopped) for garnish

Directions

Prepare Flaxseed Mixture: Combine flaxseed meal and water in a small bowl. Stir well and let sit for 5 minutes to thicken, creating a flax "egg" substitute.

Cook Vegetables: Heat olive oil in a skillet over medium heat. Add chopped onion, garlic, carrot, and celery. Sauté for 5-7 minutes until softened and fragrant.

Blend the Base: In a large mixing bowl, combine cooked lentils, oats, flax "egg," sautéed vegetables, tomato paste, soy sauce, and all the spices. Stir until well combined. Mash the mixture slightly with a fork or potato masher for a finer texture.

Shape and Bake: Transfer the mixture into a loaf pan lined with parchment paper, pressing it down firmly to compact.

Bake: Preheat oven to 375°F (190°C). Bake the loaf for 35-40 minutes or until firm and slightly browned on top.

Optional Topping: In the last 10 minutes of baking, spread a thin layer of tomato ketchup or BBQ sauce over the top for extra flavor.

Serve: Let the loaf rest for 10 minutes before slicing. Garnish with fresh parsley and serve with roasted vegetables, mashed potatoes, or a side salad for a complete meal.

Nutritional Information (Per Serving):

Calories: 180 | Protein: 9g | Carbs: 30g | Fats: 5g
Fiber: 7g | Cholesterol: 0mg | Sodium: 350mg | Potassium: 550mg

Jackfruit BBQ Pulled Pork Smoky and Tender Alternative

Prep. time: 10 min   Cook time: 35 min   Serves: 4

Ingredients

Young green jackfruit (canned in brine, drained, and shredded) 2 cans (14 oz each)

olive oil one tablespoon

yellow onion (chopped) 1 medium

garlic cloves (minced) 2

smoked paprika, one teaspoon

ground cumin 1/2 teaspoon

Ground black pepper 1/4 teaspoon

tomato paste two tablespoons

apple cider vinegar, one tablespoon

Maple syrup one tablespoon

soy sauce or tamari, one tablespoon

liquid smoke 1/2 teaspoon

BBQ sauce (plant-based) 1/2 cup

salt to taste

Optional Toppings

coleslaw (plant-based) for topping

fresh cilantro (chopped) for garnish

sliced pickles

Directions

Prepare Jackfruit: Drain and rinse the jackfruit thoroughly. Use your hands or two forks to shred the jackfruit into small pieces, removing any seeds.

Sauté Vegetables: Heat olive oil over medium heat in a large skillet. Add chopped onion and garlic, sautéing for 5 minutes until softened.

Season: Add smoked paprika, cumin, black pepper, and salt to the skillet. Stir well to coat the onions and garlic with the spices.

Simmer Jackfruit: Add the shredded jackfruit to the skillet along with tomato paste, apple cider vinegar, maple syrup, soy sauce, and liquid smoke. Stir well to combine. Let it cook over medium-low heat for 15-20 minutes, stirring occasionally, until the jackfruit absorbs the flavors and becomes tender.

Add BBQ Sauce: Stir in the BBQ sauce and simmer for 5-7 minutes, allowing the jackfruit to soak up the sauce and become fully coated.

Serve: The BBQ-pulled jackfruit should be served on a toasted bun with a generous scoop of plant-based coleslaw, fresh cilantro, and pickles for added crunch.

Nutritional Information (Per Serving):

Calories: 180 | Protein: 3g | Carbs: 35g | Fats: 6g
Fiber: 5g | Cholesterol: 0mg | Sodium: 700mg | Potassium: 500mg

Tempeh Bacon Bliss Crispy Smoky Breakfast Favorite

Prep. time: 10 min   Setting Time: 20 minutes   Serves: 4
(marinating)
Cooking Time: 10 minutes

Ingredients

tempeh (sliced thinly) 8 oz
soy sauce or tamari, three tablespoons
Maple syrup one tablespoon
liquid smoke, one teaspoon
apple cider vinegar, one teaspoon
smoked paprika, one teaspoon
garlic powder 1/2 teaspoon
black pepper pinch
olive oil one tablespoon
Optional Toppings
avocado slices for serving
sliced tomatoes
fresh basil leaves

Directions

Marinate Tempeh: In a shallow dish, mix soy sauce, maple syrup, liquid smoke, apple cider vinegar, smoked paprika, garlic powder, and black pepper. Lay the tempeh slices in the marinade, ensuring they are fully coated. Let sit for 20 minutes, flipping halfway through.

Cook Tempeh: Heat olive oil in a large skillet over medium heat. Add the marinated tempeh slices in a single layer. Cook for 3-4 minutes on each side until crispy and browned.

Serve: Serve warm as a breakfast side or layer in a sandwich with avocado slices, tomatoes, and fresh basil for a flavorful start to the day.

Nutritional Information (Per Serving):

Calories: 180 | Protein: 9g | Carbs: 14g | Fats: 10g
Fiber: 3g | Cholesterol: 0mg | Sodium: 600mg | Potassium: 250mg

Chickpea Nuggets Crispy Bites for Kids and Adults Alike

Prep. time: 10 min   Setting Time: 15 minutes   Serves: 4
Cooking Time: 20 minutes

Ingredients

cooked chickpeas 1 1/2 cups
rolled oats 1/2 cup
nutritional yeast two tablespoons
garlic powder, one teaspoon
onion powder, one teaspoon
paprika 1/2 teaspoon
salt 1/2 teaspoon
black pepper pinch
plant-based milk 1/4 cup
olive oil one tablespoon (optional for baking)
Optional Toppings
Serve with ketchup, hummus, or a vegan ranch dip.
Sprinkle with sesame seeds for added texture.

Directions

Blend Ingredients: In a food processor, combine chickpeas, rolled oats, nutritional yeast, garlic powder, onion powder, paprika, salt, and black pepper. Pulse until the mixture forms a sticky, cohesive dough. Add plant-based milk and blend briefly to combine.

Shape Nuggets: Scoop 1-2 tablespoons of the mixture and shape it into nuggets-sized pieces. Place them on a lined baking sheet and chill in the refrigerator for 15 minutes to firm up.

Bake or Pan-Fry: Preheat the oven to 375°F (190°C) or heat a skillet over medium heat with olive oil. For baking, lightly brush the nuggets with olive oil and bake for 20 minutes, flipping halfway through. For frying, cook each side for 3-4 minutes until golden and crispy.

Serve: Serve warm with your favorite dipping sauces or in a wrap for a wholesome meal.

Nutritional Information (Per Serving):

Calories: 180 | Protein: 6g | Carbs: 20g | Fats: 6g
Fiber: 4g | Cholesterol: 0mg | Sodium: 400mg | Potassium: 250mg

Walnut and Mushroom Beef, a Savory Crumble for Tacos or Pasta

Prep. time: 10 min   Total time: 15 min   Serves: 4

Ingredients

walnuts 1 cup (soaked for 15 minutes and drained)
button or cremini mushrooms 2 cups (finely chopped)
onion one small (diced)
garlic two cloves (minced)
soy sauce or tamari, two tablespoons
smoked paprika, one teaspoon
ground cumin one teaspoon
olive oil one tablespoon
salt and black pepper to taste
Optional Toppings
chopped fresh cilantro for tacos
grated vegan cheese for pasta
Drizzle of vegan sour cream or hot sauce

Directions

Prepare Walnuts: Soak walnuts in warm water for 15 minutes to soften. Drain and pulse in a food processor until crumbly but not pasty.
Sauté Vegetables: Heat olive oil in a large skillet over medium heat. Add onions and garlic, cooking until translucent. Add mushrooms and cook for 5-7 minutes until softened and liquid has evaporated.
Combine Ingredients: Stir in walnut crumbles, soy sauce, smoked paprika, cumin, salt, and pepper. Cook for another 5 minutes, stirring occasionally, until flavors meld and mixture resembles ground meat.
Serve: The walnut-mushroom crumble can be used as a filling for tacos, a topping for pasta, or even a layer in a plant-based shepherd's pie.

Nutritional Information (Per Serving):

Calories: 180 | Protein: 5g | Carbs: 8g | Fats: 15g
Fiber: 3g | Cholesterol: 0mg | Sodium: 400mg | Potassium: 350mg

Seitan Sausage Patties Spiced Perfection for Any Meal

Prep. time: 15 min   Cook time: 15 min   Serves: 6

Ingredients

vital wheat gluten 1 cup
chickpea flour 1/4 cup
vegetable broth 3/4 cup (warm)
soy sauce, two tablespoons
olive oil one tablespoon
smoked paprika, one teaspoon
ground fennel seeds, one teaspoon
ground sage one teaspoon
garlic powder, one teaspoon
onion powder, one teaspoon
black pepper 1/2 teaspoon
red pepper flakes 1/4 teaspoon (optional, for heat)
Optional Toppings
vegan gravy for a hearty meal
Maple syrup drizzle for a sweet-savory breakfast

Directions

Mix Dry Ingredients: Combine vital wheat gluten, chickpea flour, smoked paprika, fennel seeds, sage, garlic powder, onion powder, black pepper, and red pepper flakes in a large bowl.
Prepare Wet Ingredients: In a small bowl, whisk together warm vegetable broth, soy sauce, and olive oil.
Form Dough: Gradually add wet and dry ingredients, stirring until the dough forms. Knead for 2-3 minutes until firm and elastic.
Shape Patties: Divide the dough into six equal portions and flatten each into a patty.
Cook Patties: Heat a non-stick skillet over medium heat. Cook patties for 5-7 minutes per side until golden brown and slightly crisp.
Serve: Patties are a protein addition to breakfast sandwiches, alongside roasted vegetables or any meal.

Nutritional Information (Per Serving):

Calories: 180 | Protein: 18g | Carbs: 10g | Fats: 5g
Fiber: 2g | Cholesterol: 0mg | Sodium: 400mg | Potassium: 250mg

Cashew Cream Cheese Smooth and Spreadable Delight

Prep. time: 10 min   Setting Time: 2 hours (soaking)   Serves: 8 (about 1 1/2 cups)

Ingredients
raw cashews 1 cup (soaked for 2 hours or overnight)
lemon juice, two tablespoons
apple cider vinegar, one tablespoon
nutritional yeast one tablespoon
Water 3-4 tablespoons (adjust for consistency)
sea salt 1/2 teaspoon
Optional Toppings and Variations
Mix in fresh herbs like chives or dill for a savory flavor.
Add one teaspoon of garlic powder or roasted garlic for extra depth.
Blend with a tablespoon of maple syrup for a sweet spread.

Directions
Soak Cashews: For a creamier texture, soak raw cashews in water for 2 hours or overnight. Drain and rinse before use.
Blend Ingredients: Add soaked cashews, lemon juice, apple cider vinegar, nutritional yeast, water, and sea salt to a high-speed blender or food processor. Blend until smooth, stopping to scrape down sides as needed.
Adjust Consistency: Add more water, one tablespoon at a time, until desired creaminess is reached.
Flavor Variations: Mix herbs, garlic, or other desired flavorings and pulse to combine.
Chill and Serve: Transfer to a container and refrigerate for 1 hour to firm up. Serve as a spread on bagels or crackers or as a dip for vegetables.

Nutritional Information (Per Serving):
Calories: 110 | Protein: 3g | Carbs: 5g | Fats: 9g
Fiber: 1g | Cholesterol: 0mg | Sodium: 120mg | Potassium: 150mg

Almond Parmesan Crumble Nutty Cheesy and Dairy-Free

Prep. time: 5 min   Total time: 5 min   Serves: 10 (about 1 1/4 cups)

Ingredients
raw almonds 1 cup
nutritional yeast, three tablespoons
sea salt 1/2 teaspoon
garlic powder 1/2 teaspoon
Optional Toppings and Variations
Add 1/2 teaspoon smoked paprika for a smoky flavor.
Mix in 1 tablespoon of dried Italian herbs for added depth.
Cashews or sunflower seeds should be used instead of almonds for a different taste and texture.

Directions
Prepare Ingredients: Ensure almonds are raw and unsalted for optimal flavor and nutrition.
Blend Ingredients: Combine almonds, nutritional yeast, sea salt, and garlic powder in a food processor or blender. Pulse until the mixture forms a coarse, crumbly texture resembling grated Parmesan. Avoid over-blending to keep it light and crumbly.
Adjust Flavor: Taste the crumble and add more salt or nutritional yeast to suit your preferences.
Store: Transfer to an airtight container and store in the refrigerator for up to two weeks.
Serve: Sprinkle over pasta, salads, roasted vegetables, or soups as a savory topping.

Nutritional Information (Per Serving):
Calories: 100 | Protein: 3g | Carbs: 3g | Fats: 9g
Fiber: 2g | Cholesterol: 0mg | Sodium: 100mg | Potassium: 120mg

Mozza-Magic Stretchy Vegan Mozzarella for Pizza Night

Prep. time: 10 min   Setting time: 5 min   Serves: 4

Ingredients

raw cashews 1/2 cup (soaked for 4 hours or boiled for 10 minutes)
tapioca starch three tablespoons
unsweetened almond milk 1 cup
nutritional yeast two tablespoons
apple cider vinegar, one teaspoon
lemon juice, one teaspoon
sea salt 1/2 teaspoon
garlic powder 1/4 teaspoon
Optional Toppings and Variations
Add a pinch of smoked paprika for a smoky flavor.
Include 1/2 teaspoon of onion powder for extra depth.
Blend in 1 tablespoon of olive oil for a richer texture.

Directions

Soak Cashews: Drain and rinse soaked cashews to remove excess starch and ensure a creamy base.
Blend Ingredients: Combine cashews, tapioca starch, almond milk, nutritional yeast, apple cider vinegar, lemon juice, sea salt, and garlic powder in a blender. Blend until smooth and creamy.
Cook and Thicken: Pour the mixture into a saucepan and heat over medium heat, stirring constantly with a spatula or whisk. As the mixture heats, it will begin to thicken and turn stretchy. This process typically takes 3–5 minutes.
Test Consistency: Remove from heat once it reaches a stretchy, gooey texture. Adjust seasoning if necessary.
Serve: Use immediately as a topping for pizza, sandwiches, or pasta. For later use, refrigerate and reheat gently to regain its stretchy texture.

Nutritional Information (Per Serving):
Calories: 120 | Protein: 4g | Carbs: 9g | Fats: 8g
Fiber: 1g | Cholesterol: 0mg | Sodium: 200mg | Potassium: 150mg

Smoky Gouda-Style Cheese Creamy Block for Slicing and Melting

Prep. time: 15 min   Setting Time: 2 hours   Serves: 8

Ingredients

raw cashews 1 cup (soaked for 4 hours or boiled for 10 minutes)
unsweetened almond milk 1 1/4 cups
tapioca starch three tablespoons
nutritional yeast 1/4 cup
agar-agar powder two teaspoons
apple cider vinegar two teaspoons
liquid smoke, one teaspoon
smoked paprika 1/2 teaspoon
onion powder 1/2 teaspoon
garlic powder 1/4 teaspoon
sea salt 1/2 teaspoon
Optional Toppings and Variations
Add chopped chives or dill for a herby flavor.
Blend in 1 tablespoon of olive oil for extra richness.

Directions

Soak Cashews: Drain and rinse soaked cashews to ensure a smooth, creamy texture.
Blend Ingredients: In a blender, combine cashews, almond milk, tapioca starch, nutritional yeast, apple cider vinegar, liquid smoke, smoked paprika, onion powder, garlic powder, and sea salt. Blend until completely smooth.
Prepare Agar Mixture: Combine 1/2 cup almond milk and agar-agar powder in a small saucepan. Heat over medium heat, whisking constantly, until the mixture boils and thickens. This activates the agar for a firm cheese block.
Combine Mixtures: Pour the blended cashew mixture into the saucepan with the agar mixture. Stir continuously over medium heat until the mixture becomes thick and glossy, about 3–5 minutes.
Set the Cheese: Transfer the mixture into a lightly oiled mold or dish. Smooth the top with a spatula. Let it cool at room temperature for 15 minutes, then refrigerate for at least 2 hours until fully set.
Serve: Slice or melt the cheese as desired. Perfect for sandwiches, crackers, or pizza.

Nutritional Info (Per Serving):
Calories: 160 | Protein: 4g | Carbs: 12g | Fats: 10g
Fiber: 2g | Cholesterol: 0mg | Sodium: 300mg | Potassium: 200mg

Part 3: Meal Planning and Prep

3.1. Beginner Meal Plans

28-day meal plan for easy plant-based eating.

Transitioning to a plant-based diet can be an exciting journey filled with vibrant flavors, diverse ingredients, and numerous health benefits. However, for beginners, meal planning can sometimes feel overwhelming. That's where a structured 28-day meal plan comes in handy.

This meal plan simplifies your week and makes incorporating wholesome, plant-based meals into your daily routine easier. By following this plan, you'll discover how easy it is to prepare delicious and nutritious dishes that satisfy your taste buds and nourish your body.

Each day features a balanced selection of breakfasts, lunches, and dinners, ensuring you receive various nutrients while enjoying the rich diversity of plant-based foods. From hearty grains and legumes to fresh fruits and vegetables, this meal plan will help you explore new recipes and flavors, making your transition to a plant-based lifestyle enjoyable and sustainable.

One significant advantage of a well-planned meal routine is the ability to repurpose leftovers. If you have extra servings from breakfast or lunch, don't hesitate to enjoy them the next day! This saves time, reduces food waste, and ensures you get the most out of the delicious meals you've prepared.

Leftovers can be a lifesaver on busy days when you need something quick and nourishing. To keep your leftovers fresh and flavorful:

Store Properly: Use airtight containers to preserve taste and texture.

Reheat Gently: Warm up meals on the stovetop or microwave, adding a splash of water or plant-based milk to maintain moisture.

Get Creative: Leftovers can also be transformed—use roasted veggies from dinner as a topping for a grain bowl or blend leftover soups into a hearty sauce.

Incorporating leftovers into your meal plan gives you flexibility and helps you stay consistent. Enjoy the convenience and savor every bite, knowing that a little extra today makes tomorrow even easier!

28-Day Plant-Based Meal Plan: Week 1

Week 1	Monday	Tuesday	Wednesday	Tuesday	Friday	Saturday	Sunday
Breakfast	Overnight Chia Pudding with Fresh Berries	Avocado and Tomato Breakfast Toast	5-Minute Banana Oat Pancakes	Plant-Based Breakfast Burrito with Tofu Scramble	Creamy Coconut Yogurt Parfaits	High-Protein Peanut Butter Smoothie Bowl	Golden Glow Turmeric Spiced Oats
Snack	No-Bake Energy Bites with Dates and Cacao	Berry Blast Protein Smoothie	Crispy Baked Chickpeas with Spices	Decadent Chocolate Peanut Butter Smoothie	Air-Fried Sweet Potato Wedges	Tropical Pineapple Coconut Protein Smoothie	Garlic and Herb Kale Chips
Lunch	Mediterranean Hummus Wrap	Easy Chickpea Salad Sandwich	Sweet Potato and Black Bean Tacos	Protein-Packed Mason Jar Salad	Quick Curry Lentil Rice Bowls	Grilled Veggie and Quinoa Buddha Bowl	Vegan Caesar Salad Wrap
Soup/Salad	Creamy Coconut Tomato Soup	Fresh Kale and Quinoa Power Bowl.	Rainbow Chickpea Salad with Lemon Dressing	Spiced Sweet Potato and Carrot Soup	Zesty Citrus and Arugula Salad with Walnuts	Smoky Black Bean and Corn Salad	Crunchy Asian Slaw with Sesame Ginger Dressing
Dinner	Spicy Coconut Lentil Curry	One-Pot Garlic and Herb Orzo with Vegetables	Zucchini Noodles with Pesto and Cherry Tomatoes	Creamy Vegan Spinach and Artichoke Pasta	Hearty Black Bean and Sweet Potato Chili	Plant-Based Shepherd's Pie	Smoky Eggplant and Chickpea Stew
Dessert	Vegan S'mores Bars with Almond Butter	Flourless Peanut Butter Cookies	Chocolate Avocado Mousse	Pumpkin Spice Vegan Cupcakes	Fresh Berry Vegan Cheesecake Bars	Maple Cinnamon Roasted Pears with Walnuts	Sweet Potato and Chocolate Chip Blondies

28-Day Plant-Based Meal Plan: Week 2

Week 2	Monday	Tuesday	Wednesday	Tuesday	Friday	Saturday	Sunday
Breakfast	Golden Glow Turmeric Spiced Oats	Creamy Coconut Yogurt Parfaits	Savory Sweet Potato Breakfast Hash	5-Minute Banana Oat Pancakes	Plant-Based Breakfast Burrito with Tofu Scramble	Overnight Chia Pudding with Fresh Berries	Quick Tropical Green Smoothie
Snack	Berry Blast Protein Smoothie	Crispy Baked Chickpeas with Spices	Classic Plant-Based Trail Mix	Garlic and Herb Kale Chips	Tropical Pineapple Coconut Protein Smoothie	Decadent Chocolate Peanut Butter Smoothie	No-Bake Energy Bites with Dates and Cacao
Lunch	Mediterranean Hummus Wrap	Sweet Potato and Black Bean Tacos	Protein-Packed Mason Jar Salad	Grilled Veggie and Quinoa Buddha Bowl	Zesty Lime and Cilantro Rice Burrito Bowls	Creamy Avocado Chickpea Stuffed Pita	Quick Curry Lentil Rice Bowls
Soup/Salad	Creamy Coconut Tomato Soup	Crunchy Asian Slaw with Sesame Ginger Dressing	Rustic White Bean and Kale Soup	Mediterranean Orzo Salad with Fresh Herbs	Rainbow Chickpea Salad with Lemon Dressing	Spiced Sweet Potato and Carrot Soup	Spiced Sweet Potato and Carrot Soup
Dinner	Spicy Coconut Lentil Curry	Creamy Vegan Mushroom Stroganoff	Zucchini Noodles with Pesto and Cherry Tomatoes	Smoky Vegan Sloppy Joes	Thai Green Curry with Tofu and Veggies	Smoky Eggplant and Chickpea Stew	Plant-Based Shepherd's Pie
Dessert	Fresh Berry Vegan Cheesecake Bars	Flourless Peanut Butter Cookies	Chocolate Avocado Mousse	No-Bake Vegan Lemon Tarts	Decadent Vegan Chocolate Brownies	Pumpkin Spice Vegan Cupcakes	Sweet Potato and Chocolate Chip Blondies

28-Day Plant-Based Meal Plan: Week 3

Week 3	Monday	Tuesday	Wednesday	Tuesday	Friday	Saturday	Sunday
Breakfast	Savory Sweet Potato Breakfast Hash	Quick Tropical Green Smoothie	Instant Pot Steel-Cut Oats with Maple and Walnuts	High-Protein Peanut Butter Smoothie Bowl	Fluffy Vegan Apple Cinnamon Muffins	Golden Glow Turmeric Spiced Oats	Avocado and Tomato Breakfast Toast
Snack	Tropical Pineapple Coconut Protein Smoothie	Spicy Black Bean Dip with Lime	Berry Blast Protein Smoothie	Classic Plant-Based Trail Mix	Creamy Mango Lassi (Dairy-Free)	No-Bake Energy Bites with Dates and Cacao	Spicy Black Bean Dip with Lime
Lunch	Italian-inspired marinated Tempeh Wrap	Roasted Veggie and Pesto Pasta Salad	Zesty Lime and Cilantro Rice Burrito Bowls	Spicy Soba Noodle Bento Box	Mediterranean Hummus Wrap	Hearty Barbecue Jackfruit Sliders	Sweet Potato and Black Bean Tacos
Soup/Salad	Thai-Inspired Peanut Noodle Salad	Mediterranean Orzo Salad with Fresh Herbs	15-minute Tomato Basil Gazpacho	Crunchy Asian Slaw with Sesame Ginger Dressing	Fresh Kale and Quinoa Power Bowl	Zesty Citrus and Arugula Salad with Walnuts	Rainbow Chickpea Salad with Lemon Dressing
Dinner	Creamy Vegan Mushroom Stroganoff	Cheesy Baked Cauliflower Casserole	Crispy Baked Cauliflower Tacos	Warm and Cheesy Vegan Garlic Breadsticks with Creamy Tomato Soup	Vegan Sloppy Joes with Dairy-Free Mashed Potatoes	Smoky Vegan Lasagna with Cashew Ricotta	Creamy Vegan Spinach and Artichoke Pasta
Dessert	Apple Cinnamon Crumble with Oat Topping	Raspberry Chia Jam Thumbprint Cookies	Decadent Vegan Chocolate Brownies	Sweet Potato and Chocolate Chip Blondies	Chocolate-Dipped Coconut Macaroons	Vegan Cheesecake Bars	Chocolate Avocado Mousse

28-Day Plant-Based Meal Plan: Week 4

Week 4	Monday	Tuesday	Wednesday	Tuesday	Friday	Saturday	Sunday
Breakfast	Overnight Chia Pudding with Fresh Berries	Creamy Coconut Yogurt Parfaits	5-Minute Banana Oat Pancakes	Savory Sweet Potato Breakfast Hash	Quick Tropical Green Smoothie	Plant-Based Breakfast Burrito with Tofu Scramble	High-Protein Peanut Butter Smoothie Bowl
Snack	Air-Fried Sweet Potato Wedges	Garlic and Herb Kale Chips	Tropical Pineapple Coconut Protein Smoothie	Classic Plant-Based Trail Mix	Spicy Peanut Sauce with Veggie Sticks	Decadent Chocolate Peanut Butter Smoothie	No-Bake Energy Bites with Dates and Cacao
Lunch	Grilled Veggie and Quinoa Buddha Bowl	Easy Chickpea Salad Sandwich	Quick Curry Lentil Rice Bowls	Creamy Avocado Chickpea Stuffed Pita	Zesty Lime and Cilantro Rice Burrito Bowls	Sweet Potato and Black Bean Tacos	Spicy Soba Noodle Bento Box
Soup/Salad	Smoky Black Bean and Corn Salad	Spiced Sweet Potato and Carrot Soup	Crunchy Asian Slaw with Sesame Ginger Dressing	Mediterranean Orzo Salad with Fresh Herbs	Fresh Kale and Quinoa Power Bowl	Rainbow Chickpea Salad with Lemon Dressing	Creamy Avocado and Spinach Salad
Dinner	Thai Green Curry with Tofu and Veggies	Balsamic Glazed Roasted Veggie and Quinoa Bowl	Plant-Based Shepherd's Pie	Creamy Vegan Mushroom Stroganoff	Smoky Eggplant and Chickpea Stew	Crispy Baked Cauliflower Tacos	Hearty Black Bean and Sweet Potato Chili
Dessert	Flourless Peanut Butter Cookies	Pumpkin Spice Vegan Cupcakes	No-Bake Vegan Lemon Tarts	Apple Cinnamon Crumble with Oat Topping	Vegan Cheesecake Bars	Raspberry Chia Jam Thumbprint Cookies	Decadent Vegan Chocolate Brownies

3.2. Meal Prep Tips

How to batch cook and save time.

Batch cooking is a game-changer for anyone looking to save time, reduce stress, and stay consistent with a plant-based lifestyle. By preparing larger quantities of food in advance, you'll have nutritious meals ready throughout the week. Here are some practical tips and strategies to make batch cooking efficient and enjoyable

Plan Ahead

Use a Weekly Menu: Select recipes that work well for meal prep, such as soups, stews, casseroles, salads, and grain bowls.

Grocery Shop with a List: Knowing precisely what you'll cook prevents overbuying and ensures you have all the necessary ingredients.

Choose Batch-Friendly Recipes

Opt for dishes that store well in the fridge or freezer without losing flavor or texture, such as lentil stews, roasted vegetables, and grains like quinoa or rice.

Prepare versatile components like sauces, dips, and dressings that can be used in multiple meals.

Use Your Time Wisely

Cook in Bulk: Double or triple recipes to create extra servings for future meals.

Multitask: Use the oven, stovetop, and Instant Pot simultaneously to prepare several dishes simultaneously—for example, roast vegetables while simmering soup and cooking grains.

Prep Ingredients in Advance: To streamline your cooking session, chop vegetables, soak beans, or prepare marinades the night before.

Invest in Storage Solutions

Airtight Containers: Store cooked meals and ingredients in reusable glass or BPA-free plastic containers to keep cooked meals fresh.

Portion-Control Containers: Divide meals into individual servings for easy grab-and-go options.

Freezer-friendly bags or Containers: These can be used for soups, stews, and sauces to keep them fresh for weeks or months.

Organize Your Kitchen

Designate a specific day and time for batch cooking, such as Sunday afternoons.

Maximize Freezer Use

Many plant-based foods freeze well, including cooked grains, beans, soups, and chopped vegetables. To avoid confusion, label containers with the name and date.

For a quick breakfast, freeze items like smoothie packs (pre-portioned fruit, spinach, and seeds).

Prep Key Ingredients

Cook Grains in Bulk: Prepare a large batch of quinoa, rice, or farro to use as the base for multiple meals.

Roast Vegetables: Roast various veggies to mix and match with meals throughout the week.

Prepare Legumes: Cook a big batch of beans or lentils for salads, stews, or tacos.

Reimagine Leftovers

Transform roasted vegetables into wraps or grain bowls.

Use leftover soups as a base for new dishes by adding fresh ingredients.

Blend extra greens and herbs into dips, dressings, or sauces to reduce waste.

Simplify with Theme Nights

To streamline meal planning and batch prep, assign themes like "Soup Sunday," "Taco Tuesday," or "Salad Saturday."

Make one large batch of a themed dish to enjoy for dinner and leftovers

Make It a Habit

Batch cooking saves time and ensures you always have healthy options on hand. Incorporating this practice into your weekly routine will reduce stress, save money, and keep you motivated on your plant-based journey.

With some planning and preparation, batch cooking can be your secret weapon for sticking to a plant-based lifestyle while making your busy life easier and more enjoyable.

Freezer-friendly meals and storage tips.

Freezing meals is an excellent way to save time, reduce waste, and ensure you always have nutritious, plant-based options. With proper storage techniques and meal preparation strategies, your freezer can become your best friend in maintaining a healthy, plant-based lifestyle. Here's everything you need to know about creating and storing freezer-friendly meals:

Choosing Freezer-Friendly Meals

Not all meals freeze equally well, so focus on dishes that maintain their texture and flavor after freezing.

Great Options:

Soups and Stews: Lentil soups, chili, or creamy butternut squash soup are ideal for freezing.

Casseroles and Bakes: Lasagna, shepherd's pie, or baked pasta dishes reheat beautifully.

Grains and Legumes: Cooked quinoa, rice, beans, and lentils are perfect staples to freeze for quick meal assembly.

Veggie Burgers and Patties: Plant-based burger patties or falafel freeze well and are easy to reheat.

Sauces and Dips: Pesto, hummus, and marinara sauce can be frozen in small portions for future use.

Preparation Tips for Freezing Meals

Cool Before Freezing: To prevent ice crystals from forming, let your meals cool completely before placing them in the freezer.

Portion Control: Divide meals into single-serving portions to make reheating easier and reduce waste.

Avoid Freezing Fresh Greens: Leafy greens like spinach or lettuce lose their texture when frozen. Instead, add them fresh to meals.

Leave Room for Expansion: Liquid-based meals like soups expand when frozen, so leave about an inch of space at the top of the container.

Inspiration and Final Words

Embarking on a plant-based lifestyle is a journey of discovery, growth, and self-care. Whether you're just beginning or deepening your commitment to plant-based eating, every step you take is worth celebrating. Small changes add to significant progress; each meal is an opportunity to nourish your body, care for the planet, and honor your values.

Celebrate Your Progress

Progress is not about perfection—it's about consistency and intention. Celebrate whenever you choose a plant-based meal, try a new recipe, or learn something new about this lifestyle. Progress may look like swapping out dairy for almond milk, preparing your first plant-based dinner for friends, or sticking to your meal plan during a busy week. Recognize and embrace these victories—they are the foundation of lasting change.

The Long-Term Health Benefits of Plant-Based Eating

Adopting a plant-based lifestyle offers profound health benefits, not only for your body but also for your mind. Over time, you'll experience:

Improved Physical Health:
A plant-based diet is rich in nutrients, antioxidants, and fiber, which help reduce the risk of chronic diseases like heart disease, diabetes, and certain cancers. Focusing on whole foods like fruits, vegetables, legumes, and grains can lower blood pressure, improve cholesterol levels, and maintain a healthy weight.

Increased Energy:
A diet rich in plant-based foods provides your body with a steady supply of clean, natural energy. The absence of heavy animal products can help you feel more energized throughout the day, improving focus and reducing fatigue.

Stronger Immune System:
Plant-based eating supports an immune system due to plant foods' abundance of vitamins, minerals, and phytonutrients. These nutrients help your body fight infections, repair tissues, and maintain well-being.

Mental Clarity and Emotional Balance:
Many people experience improved mental clarity and emotional well-being on a plant-based diet. Nutrient-rich foods promote brain health and stabilize blood sugar levels, contributing to more balanced moods, better focus, and reduced anxiety.

By embracing a plant-based diet, you're nourishing your body and creating a lifestyle that supports long-term health and mental clarity, leaving you feeling better inside and out.

Keep Exploring and Growing

Remember, plant-based eating is not about deprivation but abundance. A world of flavors, cuisines, and ingredients is waiting to be discovered. Continue to experiment, adapt recipes, and share your journey with others. Each step inspires those around you and contributes to a broader movement toward a healthier, more sustainable future.

You're Not Alone

This cookbook is just the beginning. There's a vibrant community of plant-based enthusiasts worldwide who share tips, support, and inspiration. Connecting with others can make the journey more enjoyable and rewarding, whether online or in your local area.

Here's to your continued progress and the countless delicious, plant-based meals ahead.

If you've enjoyed this book and found it helpful in your plant-based journey, I'd be so grateful if you could take a moment to leave a review on Amazon. Your feedback helps others discover this cookbook and encourages me to continue creating content that supports your plant-based lifestyle. I appreciate your support!

Index Recipes

Made in the USA
Las Vegas, NV
03 January 2025

15794038R00057